100

Best Classic
Tapas

100

Best Classic
Tapas

The ultimate ingredients for authentic tapas including 100 delicious recipes

This edition published in 2012
LOVE FOOD is an imprint of Parragon Books Ltd

Parragon
Queen Street House
4 Queen Street
Bath BA1 1HE, UK

www.parragon.com

ISBN: 978-1-4454-6200-4

Printed in Indonesia

Cover photography by Mike Cooper
Photography by Günter Beer and Laurie Evans
Home economy by Stevan Paul and Carol Tennant
Internal design by Jane Bozzard-Hill
Introduction by Beverly LeBlanc

Notes for the Reader
This book uses both metric and imperial measurements. Follow the
same units of measurement throughout; do not mix metric and imperial. All spoon measurements are level: teaspoons are assumed to be
5 ml, and tablespoons are assumed to be 15 ml. Unless otherwise
stated, milk is assumed to be full fat, eggs and individual vegetables are
medium, and pepper is freshly ground black pepper.

The times given are an approximate guide only. Preparation times
differ according to the techniques used by different people and the
cooking times may also vary from those given. Optional ingredients,
variations or serving suggestions have not been included in the calcu-
lations.

Recipes using raw or very lightly cooked eggs should be avoided by
infants, the elderly, pregnant women, convalescents and anyone suffer-
ing from an illness. Pregnant and breastfeeding women are advised to
avoid eating peanuts and peanut products. Sufferers from nut allergies
should be aware that some of the ready-made ingredients used in
the recipes in this book may contain nuts. Always check the packaging
before use.

contents

Introduction

Welcome to the world of Spanish tapas culture. Tapas are small, bite-sized morsels of tasty food, like finger food, that are uniquely Spanish. Tapas are served in Spanish bars and cafés throughout the day, and the preparation, eating and enjoyment of tapas are essential parts of everyday Spanish life. It can be tempting to describe tapas as the Spanish version of French hors d'oeuvres or Mediterranean meze, but they are quite different. Unlike meze, for example, tapas are never intended to replace a proper meal, nor do they form the first course of a meal, as is the role of hors d'oeuvres.

'Tapas are a national obsession of endless variety'

The Spanish rarely drink alcohol without eating, so wherever you travel in this vast country you will find people standing at bars nibbling bite-sized meat-, poultry-, vegetable- and seafood-based tapas with their drinks, be it late morning, lunchtime, mid-afternoon or in the evening before going home for a late supper. Older Spaniards fondly remember when simple tapas – a bowl of almonds or olives, slices of bread drizzled with olive oil, or chunks of chorizo – were always served free with any drink. That tradition, unfortunately, hasn't stood the test of time, but there hasn't been any decline in the popularity of tapas themselves.

The Spanish word *tapa* means 'lid', and the nation's obsession with these flavoursome titbits began hundreds of years ago when Andalusian innkeepers used slices of bread to keep dust and bugs out of the glasses of wine and sherry provided for passing horsemen. Eventually slices of ham and cheese were added to the bread to boost trade, and tapas as we know them today were born, evolving from the arid landscape of southern Spain into a national obsession of endless variety. In fact, sampling a selection of tapas is a good overall introduction to the exciting flavours of Spanish cuisine.

Tapas bars are called *tascas*, and they are very egalitarian establishments, where wine barons, bankers and industrialists rub shoulders with farm workers, students, parents with children and even tourists. Unlike English pubs or American bars, however, the raison d'être of tapas bars puts conversations and rendezvous ahead of simply drinking. Tapas bars always have a convivial atmosphere with a background buzz of friends and neighbours meeting, greeting and chatting.

If the bar is in a tourist area you might be given a menu, often with photographs to overcome language problems, but otherwise don't expect one. Some tapas bars list the daily offerings on a chalkboard, or you make your selection from the prepared tapas displayed in glass cabinets on the bar. In most of Spain the bartender or a waiter or waitress will serve you, but in the Basque Country it is traditional for customers to help themselves.

As universal as the word 'tapas' is, not all tapas are the same, as different categories exist. *Cosas de picar*, which literally means 'little things to nibble' are the simplest, such as a bowl of salted almonds, olives or cubes of cheese. These are, of course, the easiest tapas for you to serve with drinks before dinner. *Pinchos*, however, can be a bit more substantial and are easily recognized because they are speared with flat wooden cocktail sticks called *banderillas*, which resemble the darts used in bullfighting. *Cazuelas*, a type of tapas with a sauce and often hot, are so called because they are served in the small, brown glazed earthenware dishes also called *cazuelas*. Sizzling Chilli Prawns (see page 121), Chicken Livers in Sherry Sauce (see page 92) and Broad Beans with Ham (see page 37) are examples of popular *cazuelas*. These are ideal to serve to guests with drinks before dinner when you don't want to serve a first course at the table. *Montaditos* is the word to describe slices of French bread generously topped with mayonnaise-based salads, such as potato salad, tuna salad (see page 200) or salt cod (see page 190), which are served throughout the country. Part of the popularity of this type of tapas has to be that they are inexpensive and easy to prepare. *Bocadillos*, on the other hand, are small, more conventional sandwiches with a simple filling between two slices of bread. Roast loin of pork, cured ham, spicy sausage, cheese and thin omelettes are typical fillings. *Rebozadas* are the fried fritters Spaniards are so fond of – try Courgette Fritters with a Dipping Sauce (see page 25).

7

'Tapas culture is most obvious in larger cities'

By convention tapas aren't intended to be a meal, but when you see a tapas described as a *racione*, it will be more filling than most and could be just what you are looking for at lunchtime to accompany a glass of chilled *vino blanco*.

As you look through the recipes in this book, you'll see that preparing tapas offers plenty of scope for experimentation and that they can be prepared from the simplest storecupboard ingredients (see page 11). Tapas are particularly suited to entertaining, because most can be prepared well in advance, so you can enjoy the gathering as much as your guests.

Tapas Culture

You'll find tapas in every small village or town, but the height of tapas culture is most obvious in larger cities, where the nightly pilgrimage from tapas bar to tapas bar is called *tapeo*. It's a slow, relaxed procession as friends congregate at one bar to catch up on the day's news over a small glass of *fino* sherry, wine or a chilled draught beer with, perhaps, a crisp, deep-fried salt-cod fritter or a slice of tortilla, before casually meandering on to the next bar for more conversation, another drink and perhaps a few cubes of sizzling chorizo or fried, batter-coated squid rings. It's all part of the ebb and flow of the evening that a bar can be packed like a sardine can and then be virtually empty 30 minutes later, before filling up again.

Of course, regional specialities change as you travel across the country, but some tapas you will find everywhere include Spanish tortilla, a thick potato omelette; crisp, deep-fried croquettes; wafer-thin slices of Serrano ham and bowls of salted, toasted almonds or olives.

Seville and the other Andalusian cities of Granada, Cadiz and Cordoba have a lively tapas tradition, but the *tapeo* is also part of living and working in Madrid and San Sebastian. The small, winding streets behind Madrid's Plaza Mayor are where the locals gather for their nightly tapas.

In the northern Basque Country all food, be it simple marinated anchovy fillets on a slice of bread or a three-course meal in a Michelin-starred restaurant, is taken seriously, very seriously indeed. Not surprisingly, tapas in the stylish city of San Sebastian are unlike those found anywhere else. For a start, the nightly bar crawl is called *txikiteo* and tapas are called *pintxos*, the Basque word for *pinchos*, because they are almost always speared with a cocktail stick. Even a slice of tortilla is served on bread with a cocktail stick securing the two ingredients together.

Bars in the oldest part of San Sebastian compete to see which can offer the most tempting selection. It's not unusual to see thirty or more platters of tapas arranged on the bar with small wooden stands, like cake stands, used to create extra space for a second layer of platters.

When you order your drink at the bar, just ask for a plate and make your selection from all the appetizing-looking morsels. For a taste of Basque cuisine, try Anchovy Rolls (see page 199), Salt Cod on Garlic Toasts (see page 190), Basque Scrambled Eggs (see page 160) and Deep-fried Green Chillies (see page 20). When you are ready to move on to the next bar, the barman will simply count the number of cocktail sticks on your plate to calculate your bill. If you want to look like a local, throw your paper napkins on the floor.

Interestingly, Barcelona, Spain's second largest city and capital of Catalonia, doesn't have a long history of tapas culture. It is only in recent years, as improved transportation and communications have blurred regional distinctions throughout the country, not just Catalonia, that large tapas bars have appeared. Look for the bars called *xampanyerias*. Once unique to Barcelona, these bars specialize in tapas and cava, the Spanish sparkling wine.

'Recreate the flavours of Spain's tapas bars at home'

One of the great joys of tapas is that they are easy to prepare and can be made using ingredients that are widely available – in fact, it is likely that you will already have many of them in your storecupboard. However, it is worth hunting out some of the more unusual items – these can be purchased from large supermarkets or delicatessens. The following ingredients will help you recreate the flavours of Spain's tapas bars at home.

Almonds *(almendras)* A bowl of blanched almonds is one of the easiest tapas you can serve, but if you want to be more ambitious, try Salted Almonds (see page 14) or Tiny Meatballs in Almond Sauce (see page 64). For freshness, buy unblanched almonds and blanch just before using – just drop the nuts in boiling water for a few minutes, then drain and refresh under cold water. Use your fingers to squeeze the nuts so they pop out of their skins.

Cheese *(queso)* Many of Spain's numerous cheeses feature in tapas selections. For a simple tapas, serve slices of Manchego, a sheep's milk cheese from La Mancha, or cubes of Cabrales, a rich blue cheese, with drinks. Croquettes are a thrifty way to make use of small pieces of leftover cheese.

Cured meats *(charcutería)* Spanish tapas cooks make great use of cured pork, lamb and beef, and anyone visiting Spain for the first time will be dazzled by the quantity of packets in supermarkets, sliced and ready for arranging on plates for serving. Serrano or mountain ham *(jamón serrano)*, perhaps the best known, features at many tapas bars – it can be served in thin slices, as a sandwich filling or on bread topped with vegetables. Plain cooked ham, *jamón cocida*, is also used in tapas. The most highly regarded cured hams are labelled as Iberico, and you'll recognize them by the hefty price. Other equally popular *charcutería* include boneless pork loin *(lomo)* and Spain's ubiquitous pork sausage, the spicy chorizo, coloured with paprika.

Garlic *(ajo)* An essential Spanish flavouring. Buy fresh and use within a month once the head has been broken into.

Olive oil *(aceite de oliva)* Spain is the world's largest olive oil producer, so it is a regular feature of Spanish cooking; butter is rarely used. Heat destroys the flavour of oil so save your best, and most expensive, extra virgin oil for uncooked dishes and cook with plain olive oil.

Paprika *(pimentón)* Made from ground, dried red peppers, paprika adds a mild or strong smoky flavour and vibrant red colour to dishes. It's one of the essential flavours of chorizo and many Spanish dishes.

Pimientos del piquillo Take a tip from Spanish cooks and always keep a jar of these grilled and skinned peppers in your cupboard. They come bottled in olive oil or brine, either whole or sliced, and take the work out of chargrilled peppers.

Pulses *(legumbres secas)* Spanish kitchen cupboards contain many jars and cans of pulses, including butter beans *(alubia de Perú)*, chickpeas *(garbanzos)* and lentils *(lentejas)*, cooked and ready to use without having to go to the trouble of overnight soaking and boiling first. Chickpeas & Chorizo (see page 79) is a typical tapas, bursting with flavours and easy to prepare.

Saffron *(azafrán)* Good-quality Spanish saffron comes from La Mancha and is expensive. Saffron Prawns with Lemon Mayonnaise (see page 122) is a good recipe to showcase the spice's unrivalled golden colour and distinctive flavour. Enhance the flavour by lightly toasting before using. Store in a sealed container.

Canned fish *(pescado enlatado)* There is a wide selection of canned fish available, including anchovies *(boquerónes)*, sardines *(sardines)* and tuna *(atún)*. Buy fish preserved in olive oil for the best flavour.

vegetables, nuts & olives

Tapas bars can be a culinary heaven for vegetable lovers in Spain, a land of serious meat eaters. This chapter contains a wealth of vegetable recipes, celebrating Spain's position as gardener to Europe. Chargrilled peppers and courgettes always add colour and flavour to tapas menus.

Spanish cooks never run out of ideas for preparing potatoes, but Patatas Bravas, so called because of the hot chilli sauce, is one of the country's favourite tapas. Try it and you'll understand why.

Finally, what could be more quintessentially Spanish than nibbling a bowl of Olives with Orange & Lemon while sipping a cold drink?

salted almonds

SERVES 6–8
as part of a tapas meal

225 g/8 oz whole almonds,
   in their skins or blanched
4 tbsp Spanish olive oil
coarse sea salt
1 tsp paprika or ground cumin
   (optional)

Preheat the oven to 180°C/350°F/Gas Mark 4. Fresh almonds in their skins are superior in taste, but blanched almonds are much more convenient. If the almonds are not blanched, place them in a large bowl, cover with boiling water for 3–4 minutes, then drain and plunge them into cold water for 1 minute. Drain them well in a sieve, then slide off the skins between your fingers. Dry the almonds well on kitchen paper.

Place the olive oil in a roasting tin and swirl it around so that it covers the base. Add the almonds and toss them in the tin so that they are evenly coated in the oil, then spread them out in a single layer.

Roast the almonds in the preheated oven for 20 minutes, or until they are light golden brown, tossing several times during the cooking. Drain the almonds on kitchen paper, then transfer them to a bowl.

While the almonds are still warm, sprinkle with plenty of sea salt and paprika, if using, and toss together to coat. Serve the almonds warm or cold. The almonds are at their best when served freshly cooked, so, if possible, cook them on the day that you plan to eat them. However, they can be stored in an airtight container for up to 3 days.

spicy cracked marinated olives

SERVES 8
as part of a tapas meal

450 g/1 lb canned or bottled
  large green Spanish olives,
  drained
4 garlic cloves, peeled
2 tsp coriander seeds
1 small lemon
4 fresh thyme sprigs
4 feathery stalks of fennel
2 small fresh red chillies
  (optional)
pepper
Spanish extra virgin olive oil

If using unstoned olives, place them on a chopping board and, using a rolling pin, bash them lightly so that they crack slightly. Alternatively, use a sharp knife to cut a lengthways slit in each olive as far as the stone. Using the flat side of a broad knife, lightly crush each garlic clove. Using a mortar and pestle, crack the coriander seeds. Cut the lemon, with its rind, into small chunks.

Place the olives, garlic, coriander seeds, lemon chunks, thyme sprigs, fennel and chillies, if using, in a large bowl and toss together. Season to taste with pepper, but you should not need to add salt as canned or bottled olives are usually salty enough. Pack the ingredients tightly into a glass jar with a lid. Pour in enough olive oil to cover the olives, then seal the jar tightly.

Leave the olives at room temperature for 24 hours, then marinate in the refrigerator for at least 1 week but preferably 2 weeks before serving. From time to time, gently give the jar a shake to re-mix the ingredients. Return the olives to room temperature and remove from the oil to serve. Provide wooden cocktail sticks for spearing the olives.

olives with orange & lemon

Dry-fry the fennel seeds and cumin seeds in a small, heavy-based frying pan, shaking the pan frequently, until they begin to pop and give off their aroma. Remove the frying pan from the heat and leave to cool.

Place the olives, orange and lemon rind, shallots, cinnamon and toasted seeds in a bowl.

Whisk the vinegar, olive oil, orange juice, mint and parsley together in a bowl and pour over the olives. Toss well, cover and leave to chill for 1–2 days before serving.

SERVES 4–6
as part of a tapas meal

2 tsp fennel seeds
2 tsp cumin seeds
225 g/8 oz green Spanish olives
225 g/8 oz black Spanish olives
2 tsp grated orange rind
2 tsp grated lemon rind
3 shallots, finely chopped
pinch of ground cinnamon
4 tbsp white wine vinegar
5 tbsp Spanish extra virgin
    olive oil
2 tbsp orange juice
1 tbsp chopped fresh mint
1 tbsp chopped fresh parsley

deep-fried green chillies

**SERVES 4–6
as part of a tapas meal**

Spanish olive oil, for frying
250 g/9 oz sweet or hot fresh
   green chillies
sea salt

Heat 7.5 cm/3 inches of olive oil in a large, heavy-based saucepan until it reaches 180–190°C/350–375°F, or until a cube of bread turns brown in 30 seconds.

Rinse the chillies and pat them very dry with kitchen paper. Drop them in the hot oil for no longer than 20 seconds, or until they turn bright green and the skins blister.

Remove with a slotted spoon and drain well on crumpled kitchen paper. Sprinkle with sea salt and serve immediately.

sautéed garlic mushrooms

SERVES 6
as part of a tapas meal

450 g/1 lb button mushrooms
5 tbsp Spanish olive oil
2 garlic cloves, finely chopped
lemon juice
salt and pepper
4 tbsp chopped fresh parsley
lemon wedges, to garnish
crusty bread, to serve

Wipe or brush clean the mushrooms, then trim the stalks. Cut any large mushrooms in half or into quarters. Heat the olive oil in a large, heavy-based frying pan. Add the garlic and fry for 30 seconds–1 minute, or until lightly browned. Add the mushrooms and sauté over a high heat, stirring frequently, until the mushrooms have absorbed all the oil in the frying pan.

Reduce the heat to low. When the juices have come out of the mushrooms, increase the heat again and sauté for 4–5 minutes, stirring frequently, until the juices have almost evaporated. Add a squeeze of lemon juice and season to taste with salt and pepper. Stir in the parsley and cook for a further 1 minute.

Transfer the sautéed mushrooms to a warmed serving dish, garnish with lemon wedges and serve piping hot or warm. Accompany with crusty bread for mopping up the juices.

courgette fritters with a dipping sauce

To make the pine kernel sauce, place the pine kernels and garlic in a food processor and process to form a purée. With the motor still running, gradually add the olive oil, lemon juice and water to form a smooth sauce. Stir in the parsley and season to taste with salt and pepper. Transfer to a serving bowl and reserve until required.

To prepare the courgettes, cut them on the diagonal into thin slices about 5 mm/¼ inch thick. Place the flour and paprika in a polythene bag and mix together. Beat the egg and milk together in a large bowl.

Add the courgette slices to the flour mixture and toss well together until coated. Shake off the excess flour. Heat the sunflower oil in a large, heavy-based frying pan to a depth of about 1 cm/½ inch. Dip the courgette slices, one at a time, into the egg mixture, then slip them into the hot oil. Fry the courgette slices, in batches in a single layer so that they do not overcrowd the frying pan, for 2 minutes, or until they are crisp and golden brown.

Using a slotted spoon, remove the courgette fritters from the frying pan and drain on kitchen paper. Continue until all the courgette slices have been fried.

Serve the courgette fritters piping hot, lightly sprinkled with sea salt, and accompanied by the pine kernel sauce for dipping.

SERVES 6–8
as part of a tapas meal

450 g/1 lb baby courgettes
3 tbsp plain flour
1 tsp paprika
1 large egg
2 tbsp milk
sunflower oil, for pan-frying
coarse sea salt

pine kernel sauce
100 g/3½ oz pine kernels
1 garlic clove, peeled
3 tbsp Spanish extra virgin
   olive oil
1 tbsp lemon juice
3 tbsp water
1 tbsp chopped fresh flat-leaf
   parsley
salt and pepper

deep-fried artichoke hearts

SERVES 4–6
as part of a tapas meal

60 g/2¼ oz self-raising flour
¼ tsp salt
¼ tsp hot or sweet smoked
   Spanish paprika
1 garlic clove, crushed
5 tbsp water
1 tbsp olive oil
juice of ½ lemon
12 small globe artichokes
sunflower or Spanish olive oil,
   for deep-frying
aïoli (see page 50), to serve

To make the batter, put the flour, salt, paprika and garlic in a large bowl and make a well in the centre. Gradually pour the water and olive oil into the well and mix in the flour mixture from the side, beating constantly, until all the flour is incorporated and a smooth batter forms. Leave to rest while preparing the artichokes.

Fill a bowl with cold water and add the lemon juice. Cut off the stalks of the artichokes. With your hands, break off all the leaves and carefully remove the choke (the mass of silky hairs) by pulling it out with your fingers or scooping it out with a spoon. Immediately put the artichoke hearts in the acidulated water to prevent discoloration.

Cook the artichoke hearts in a saucepan of boiling salted water for 15 minutes, or until tender but still firm, then drain well and pat dry with kitchen paper.

Heat the sunflower or olive oil in a deep-fat fryer to 180–190°C/350–375°F, or until a cube of bread browns in 30 seconds. Spear an artichoke heart on a cocktail stick, dip into the batter and then drop the artichoke heart and cocktail stick into the hot oil. Cook the artichoke hearts, in batches to avoid overcrowding, for 1–2 minutes until golden brown and crisp. Remove with a slotted spoon or draining basket and drain on kitchen paper.

Serve hot, accompanied by a bowl of aïoli for dipping.

marinated aubergines

SERVES 4
as part of a tapas meal

2 aubergines, halved lengthways
salt and pepper
4 tbsp Spanish olive oil
2 garlic cloves, finely chopped
2 tbsp chopped fresh parsley
1 tbsp chopped fresh thyme
2 tbsp lemon juice

Make 2–3 slashes in the flesh of the aubergine halves and place, cut-side down, in an ovenproof dish. Season to taste with salt and pepper, pour over the olive oil and sprinkle with the garlic, parsley and thyme. Cover and leave to marinate at room temperature for 2–3 hours.

Preheat the oven to 180°C/350°F/Gas Mark 4. Uncover the dish and roast the aubergines in the preheated oven for 45 minutes. Remove the dish from the oven and turn the aubergines over. Baste with the cooking juices and sprinkle with the lemon juice. Return to the oven and cook for a further 15 minutes.

Transfer the aubergines to serving plates. Spoon over the cooking juices and serve hot or warm.

pickled stuffed peppers

Cut the cheese into pieces about 1 cm/1/2 inch long. Slit the sides of the peppers and deseed, if you like. Stuff the peppers with the cheese.

Arrange the stuffed peppers on serving plates, sprinkle with the dill and season to taste with salt and pepper. Cover and chill until ready to serve.

SERVES 6
as part of a tapas meal

200 g/7 oz Cuajada cheese,
    Queso del Tietar or other
    fresh goat's cheese
400 g/14 oz pickled peppers
    or pimientos del piquillo,
    drained
1 tbsp finely chopped fresh dill
salt and pepper

stuffed cherry tomatoes

SERVES 8
as part of a tapas meal

24 cherry tomatoes

for the anchovy & olive filling
50 g/1¾ oz canned anchovy
    fillets in olive oil
8 pimiento-stuffed green
    Spanish olives, finely chopped
2 large hard-boiled eggs, finely
    chopped
pepper

for the crab mayonnaise filling
170 g/6 oz canned crabmeat,
    drained
4 tbsp mayonnaise
1 tbsp chopped fresh flat-leaf
    parsley
salt and pepper
paprika, to garnish

for the black olive &
caper filling
12 stoned black Spanish olives
3 tbsp capers
6 tbsp aïoli (see page 50)
salt and pepper

If necessary, cut and discard a very thin slice from the stalk end of each tomato to make the bases flat and stable. Cut a thin slice from the smooth end of each cherry tomato and discard. Using a serrated knife or teaspoon, loosen the pulp and seeds of each and scoop out, discarding the flesh. Turn the scooped-out tomatoes upside down on kitchen paper and leave to drain for 5 minutes.

To make the anchovy and olive filling, drain the anchovies, reserving the olive oil for later, then chop finely and place in a bowl. Add the olives and hard-boiled eggs. Pour in a trickle of the reserved olive oil to moisten the mixture, then season with pepper. (Don't add salt to season as the anchovies are salty.) Mix well together.

To make the crab mayonnaise filling, place the crabmeat, mayonnaise and parsley in a bowl and mix well together. Season the filling to taste with salt and pepper. Sprinkle with paprika before serving.

To make the black olive and caper filling, place the olives and capers on kitchen paper to drain them well, then chop finely and place in a bowl. Add the aïoli and mix well together. Season the filling to taste with salt and pepper.

Fill a piping bag fitted with a 2-cm/¾-inch plain nozzle with the filling of your choice and use to fill the hollow tomato shells. Store the cherry tomatoes in the refrigerator until ready to serve.

simmered summer vegetables

SERVES 6–8
as part of a tapas meal

1 large aubergine
4 tbsp Spanish olive oil
1 onion, thinly sliced
2 garlic cloves, finely chopped
2 courgettes, thinly sliced
1 red pepper, cored, deseeded
    and thinly sliced
1 green pepper, cored,
    deseeded and thinly sliced
8 tomatoes, peeled, deseeded
    and chopped
salt and pepper
chopped fresh flat-leaf parsley,
    to garnish
slices thick country bread,
    to serve (optional)

Cut the aubergine into 2.5-cm/1-inch cubes. Heat the oil in a large flameproof casserole, add the onion and cook over a medium heat, stirring occasionally, for 5 minutes, or until softened but not browned. Add the garlic and cook, stirring, for 30 seconds until softened.

Increase the heat to medium-high, add the aubergine cubes and cook, stirring occasionally, for 10 minutes, or until softened and beginning to brown. Add the courgettes and peppers and cook, stirring occasionally, for 10 minutes until softened. Add the tomatoes and season to taste with salt and pepper.

Bring the mixture to the boil, then reduce the heat, cover and simmer, stirring occasionally so that the vegetables do not stick to the base of the pan, for 15–20 minutes until tender. If necessary, uncover, increase the heat and cook to evaporate any excess liquid, as the mixture should be thick.

Serve hot or cold, garnished with chopped parsley and accompanied by bread slices for scooping up the vegetables, if desired.

broad beans with ham

Bring a large saucepan of salted water to the boil. Add the beans and continue to boil for 5–10 minutes until just tender. Drain and put in a bowl of cold water to stop further cooking. Unless the beans are young and tiny, peel off the outer skins.

Meanwhile, heat 1 tablespoon of the oil in a frying pan over a medium-high heat. Add the onion and fry for about 5 minutes until soft, but not brown. Add the beans.

Stir in the ham and parsley and check the seasoning; the meat is salty, so don't add salt until after tasting. Transfer to a serving bowl and drizzle with the remaining oil. Serve at room temperature with slices of French bread.

SERVES 4–6
as part of a tapas meal

salt and pepper
225 g/8 oz fresh or frozen
   shelled broad beans
2 tbsp Spanish olive oil
1 Spanish red onion, chopped
   very finely
1 slice medium-thick Serrano
   ham, chopped
finely chopped fresh parsley,
   to taste
French bread, to serve

baby leek & asparagus salad

SERVES 6
as part of a tapas meal

3 eggs
450 g/1 lb baby leeks, trimmed
225 g/8 oz fresh young
   asparagus spears, trimmed
150 ml/5 fl oz mayonnaise
2 tbsp sherry vinegar
1 garlic clove, crushed
salt and pepper
2 tbsp capers

Put the eggs in a saucepan, cover with cold water and slowly bring to the boil. Reduce the heat and simmer gently for 10 minutes. Immediately drain the eggs and rinse under cold running water to cool. Gently tap the eggs to crack the shells and leave until cold.

Meanwhile, slice the leeks and asparagus into 9-cm/3½-inch lengths. Put both the vegetables in a saucepan of boiling water, return to the boil and boil for 12 minutes until just tender. Drain and rinse under cold running water, then drain well.

Put the mayonnaise in a large bowl, add the vinegar and garlic and mix together until smooth. Season to taste with salt and pepper. Add the leeks and asparagus to the dressing and toss together until well coated. Transfer the vegetables to a serving dish, cover and chill in the refrigerator for at least 1 hour.

Just before serving, crack the shells of the eggs all over and remove them. Slice the eggs into quarters and add to the salad. Sprinkle over the capers and serve.

courgette salad
with coriander dressing

SERVES 6
as part of a tapas meal

500 g/1 lb 2 oz small courgettes
1 tsp salt
1 tbsp Spanish olive oil
1 garlic clove, crushed
50 g/1¾ oz pine kernels

for the coriander dressing
2 garlic cloves, chopped
1 tsp ground cumin
8 tbsp chopped fresh coriander
  leaves
2 tbsp chopped fresh flat-leaf
  parsley
5 tbsp Spanish extra virgin
  olive oil
2 tbsp white wine vinegar
salt and pepper

Thinly slice the courgettes lengthways. Layer the slices in a colander, sprinkling over a little salt, and set over a large plate. Leave to drain for about 1 hour.

Meanwhile, make the dressing. Put the garlic, cumin and herbs in a food processor and pulse until well mixed.

With the motor running, add 1 tablespoon of the extra virgin olive oil, drop by drop. Using a spatula, scrape down the side of the bowl. With the motor running again, very slowly add the remaining oil in a thin, steady stream until it has all been incorporated and the dressing has slightly thickened. Add the vinegar to the dressing and process for 1 minute until blended. Season to taste with salt and pepper.

When the courgettes have drained, quickly rinse the slices under cold running water, then dry well with kitchen paper or a clean tea towel. Put in a large bowl, add the olive oil and garlic and toss together lightly.

Heat a ridged griddle pan. Add the courgette slices, in batches in a single layer, and cook, turning once, for 5 minutes, or until tender. Transfer to a large serving bowl. Set aside and leave to cool slightly.

Sprinkle the pine kernels over the courgettes. If the dressing has separated, whisk it together, then drizzle some over the courgettes. Serve the courgettes accompanied by the remaining dressing in a small serving bowl.

summer salad in a tomato dressing

Put the eggs, if using, in a saucepan, cover with cold water and slowly bring to the boil. Reduce the heat and simmer gently for 10 minutes. Immediately drain the eggs and rinse under cold running water to cool. Gently tap the eggs to crack the shells and leave until cold.

Meanwhile, cut the beans into 2.5-cm/1-inch lengths. Cook in a saucepan of boiling water for 2 minutes, then drain well, rinse under cold running water and leave until cold.

To make the dressing, coarsely grate the tomatoes into a food processor, discarding the skins left in your hands. Add the garlic, oil, vinegar, paprika and sugar and process until smooth. Season to taste with salt.

Put the cooled beans in a large serving bowl. Add the tomatoes and peppers and toss the vegetables together. Drizzle the dressing over the vegetables.

Scatter the gherkins, olives and capers into the salad. Just before serving, crack the shells of the eggs all over and remove them. Slice the eggs into quarters and add to the salad.

SERVES 8
as part of a tapas meal

4 eggs (optional)
100 g/3¹/₂ oz fine green beans
500 g/1 lb 2 oz cherry or baby
    plum tomatoes
1 green pepper, cored,
    deseeded and diced
1 yellow pepper, cored,
    deseeded and diced
4 small gherkins, sliced
50 g/1³/₄ oz stoned black
    Spanish olives, halved
1 tsp capers

for the tomato dressing
6 firm tomatoes
1 garlic clove, chopped
6 tbsp Spanish extra virgin
    olive oil
3 tbsp sherry vinegar
¹/₂ tsp hot or sweet smoked
    Spanish paprika
pinch of sugar
salt

roasted pepper salad

SERVES 8
as part of a tapas meal

3 red peppers
3 yellow peppers
5 tbsp Spanish extra virgin
  olive oil
2 tbsp dry sherry vinegar or
  lemon juice
2 garlic cloves, crushed
pinch of sugar
salt and pepper
1 tbsp capers
8 small black Spanish olives
2 tbsp chopped fresh marjoram,
  plus extra sprigs to garnish

Preheat the grill. Place all the peppers on a wire rack or grill pan and cook under the hot grill for 10 minutes, turning them frequently, until their skins have blackened and blistered all over.

Remove the roasted peppers from the heat, place them in a bowl and immediately cover tightly with a clean, damp tea towel. Alternatively, place the peppers in a polythene bag. You will find that the steam helps to soften the skins and makes it easier to remove them. Leave the peppers for about 15 minutes, or until they are cool enough to handle.

Holding 1 pepper at a time over a clean bowl, use a sharp knife to make a small hole in the base and gently squeeze out the juices and reserve them. Still holding the pepper over the bowl, carefully peel off the skin with your fingers or a knife and discard it. Cut the peppers in half and remove the stem, core and seeds, then cut each pepper into neat thin strips. Arrange the pepper strips attractively on a serving dish.

Add the olive oil, sherry vinegar, garlic, sugar and salt and pepper to taste to the reserved pepper juices. Whisk together until combined, then drizzle the dressing over the salad.

Sprinkle the capers, olives and chopped marjoram over the salad, garnish with marjoram sprigs and serve at room temperature.

orange & fennel salad

SERVES 4
as part of a tapas meal

4 large, juicy oranges
1 large fennel bulb, very thinly
  sliced
1 mild white onion, finely sliced
2 tbsp Spanish extra virgin
  olive oil
12 plump black Spanish olives,
  stoned and thinly sliced
1 fresh red chilli, deseeded and
  very thinly sliced (optional)
finely chopped fresh parsley
French bread, to serve

Finely grate the rind from the oranges into a bowl and reserve. Using a small, serrated knife, remove all the white pith from the oranges, working over a bowl to catch the juices. Cut the oranges horizontally into thin slices.

Toss the orange slices with the fennel and onion slices. Whisk the olive oil into the reserved orange juice, then spoon over the oranges. Sprinkle the olive slices over the top, add the chilli, if using, then sprinkle with the orange rind and parsley. Serve with slices of French bread.

patatas bravas

To make the sauce, heat 2 tablespoons of oil in a saucepan, add the onion and cook over a medium heat, stirring occasionally, for 5 minutes, or until softened but not browned. Add the garlic and cook, stirring, for 30 seconds. Add the wine and bring to the boil. Add the tomatoes, vinegar, chillies and paprika, reduce the heat and simmer, uncovered, for 10–15 minutes until a thick sauce forms.

When the sauce is cooked, use a handheld blender to blend until smooth. Alternatively, transfer the sauce to a food processor and process until smooth. Return the sauce to the saucepan and set aside.

Do not peel the potatoes, but cut them into chunky pieces. Heat enough oil in a large frying pan to come about 2.5 cm/1 inch up the side of the pan. Add the potato pieces and cook over a medium-high heat, turning occasionally, for 10–15 minutes until golden brown. Remove with a slotted spoon, drain on kitchen paper and sprinkle with salt.

Meanwhile, gently reheat the sauce. Transfer the potatoes to a warmed serving dish and drizzle over the sauce. Serve hot, with wooden cocktail sticks to spear the potatoes.

SERVES 6
as part of a tapas meal

Spanish olive oil,
   for shallow-frying
1 onion, finely chopped
2 garlic cloves, crushed
50 ml/2 fl oz white wine or dry
   Spanish sherry
400 g/14 oz canned chopped
   tomatoes
2 tsp white or red wine vinegar
1–2 tsp crushed dried chillies
2 tsp hot or sweet smoked
   Spanish paprika
1 kg/2 lb 4 oz potatoes
salt

baby potatoes
with aïoli

SERVES 6–8
as part of a tapas meal

450 g/1 lb baby new potatoes
salt
1 tbsp chopped fresh flat-leaf
  parsley

for the aïoli
1 large egg yolk, at room
  temperature
1 tbsp white wine vinegar or
  lemon juice
2 large garlic cloves, peeled
salt and pepper
5 tbsp Spanish extra virgin
  olive oil
5 tbsp sunflower oil
1 tbsp water

To make the aïoli, place the egg yolk, vinegar or lemon juice, garlic and salt and pepper to taste in a food processor fitted with a metal blade and blend together. With the motor still running, very slowly add the olive oil, then the sunflower oil, drop by drop at first, then, when it begins to thicken, in a slow, steady stream until the sauce is thick and smooth. Alternatively, use a bowl and whisk to make the aïoli.

For this recipe, the aïoli should be quite thin to coat the potatoes. To ensure this, blend in the water to form the consistency of sauce.

To prepare the potatoes, cut them in halves or quarters to make bite-sized pieces. If they are very small, you can leave them whole. Place the potatoes in a large saucepan of cold salted water and bring to the boil. Reduce the heat and simmer for 7 minutes, or until just tender. Drain well, then transfer to a large bowl.

While the potatoes are still warm, pour over the aïoli sauce and gently toss the potatoes in it. Adding the sauce to the potatoes while they are still warm will help them to absorb the garlic flavour. Leave for 20 minutes to allow the potatoes to marinate in the sauce.

Transfer the potatoes with aïoli to a warmed serving dish, sprinkle over the parsley and salt to taste and serve warm. Alternatively, the dish can be prepared ahead and stored in the refrigerator, but return it to room temperature before serving.

potato wedges
with shallots & rosemary

SERVES 6
as part of a tapas meal

1 kg/2 lb 4 oz small potatoes
salt and pepper
6 tbsp Spanish olive oil
2 fresh rosemary sprigs
150 g/5½ oz baby shallots
2 garlic cloves, sliced

Preheat the oven to 200°C/400°F/Gas Mark 6. Peel and cut each potato into 8 thick wedges. Put the potatoes in a large saucepan of salted water and bring to the boil. Reduce the heat and simmer for 5 minutes.

Heat the oil in a large roasting tin on the hob. Drain the potatoes well and add to the roasting tin. Strip the leaves off the rosemary sprigs, finely chop and sprinkle over the potatoes.

Roast the potatoes in the preheated oven for 35 minutes, turning twice during cooking. Add the shallots and garlic and roast for a further 15 minutes until golden brown. Season to taste with salt and pepper.

Transfer to a warmed serving dish and serve hot.

meat & poultry

As Spain is a country of serious carnivores, many meat and chicken tapas are popular. The country's seemingly infinite variety of highly prized cured hams and sausages are ideal for tapas in a hurry, as a sandwich filling or chopped and used to flavour Crispy Chicken & Ham Croquettes.

When you want a tapas that is more than just one bite, take a look at the recipes in this chapter. Moroccan Chicken Kebabs, Beef Skewers with Orange & Garlic and Lamb Skewers with Lemon are examples of *pinchos*, tapas cooked on small wooden skewers, eliminating the need for knives or forks. Or try Sirloin Steak with Garlic & Sherry or Sautéed Chicken with Crispy Garlic Slices.

sirloin steak
with garlic & sherry

SERVES 6–8
as part of a tapas meal

4 sirloin steaks, about
    175–225 g/6–8 oz each and
    2.5 cm/1 inch thick
5 garlic cloves
salt and pepper
3 tbsp Spanish olive oil
125 ml/4 fl oz dry Spanish
    sherry
chopped fresh flat-leaf parsley,
    to garnish
crusty bread, to serve

Cut the steaks into 2.5-cm/1-inch cubes and put in a large, shallow dish. Slice 3 of the garlic cloves and set aside. Finely chop the remaining garlic cloves and sprinkle over the steak cubes. Season generously with pepper and mix together well. Cover and leave to marinate in the refrigerator for 1–2 hours.

Heat the oil in a large frying pan, add the garlic slices and cook over a low heat, stirring, for 1 minute, or until golden brown. Increase the heat to medium-high, add the steak cubes and cook, stirring constantly, for 2–3 minutes until browned and almost cooked to your liking.

Add the sherry and cook until it has evaporated slightly. Season to taste with salt and turn into a warmed serving dish. Garnish with chopped parsley and serve hot, accompanied by chunks or slices of crusty bread to mop up the juices.

beef skewers with orange & garlic

SERVES 6–8
as part of a tapas meal

3 tbsp white wine
2 tbsp Spanish olive oil
3 garlic cloves, finely chopped
juice of 1 orange
450 g/1 lb rump steak, cubed
salt and pepper
450 g/1 lb baby onions, halved
2 orange peppers, deseeded
  and cut into squares
225 g/8 oz cherry tomatoes,
  halved

Mix the wine, olive oil, garlic and orange juice together in a shallow, non-metallic dish. Add the cubes of beef, season to taste with salt and pepper and toss to coat. Cover with clingfilm and leave to marinate in the refrigerator for 2–8 hours.

Preheat the grill to high. Drain the beef, reserving the marinade. Thread the beef, onions, peppers and tomatoes alternately onto several small skewers.

Cook under the hot grill, turning and brushing frequently with the marinade, for 10 minutes, or until cooked through. Transfer to warmed serving plates and serve immediately.

calves' liver in almond saffron sauce

To make the sauce, heat 2 tablespoons of the oil in a large frying pan. Tear the bread into small pieces and add to the frying pan with the almonds. Cook over a low heat, stirring frequently, for 2 minutes, or until golden brown. Stir in the garlic and cook, stirring, for 30 seconds.

Add the saffron and sherry to the frying pan and season to taste with salt and pepper. Bring to the boil and continue to boil for 1–2 minutes. Remove from the heat and leave to cool slightly, then transfer the mixture to a food processor. Add the stock and process until smooth. Set aside.

Cut the liver into large bite-sized pieces. Dust lightly with flour and season generously with pepper. Heat the remaining oil in the frying pan, add the liver and cook over a medium heat, stirring constantly, for 2–3 minutes until firm and lightly browned.

Pour the sauce into the frying pan and reheat gently for 1–2 minutes. Transfer to a warmed serving dish and garnish with chopped parsley. Serve hot, accompanied by chunks of crusty bread to mop up the sauce.

SERVES 6
as part of a tapas meal

4 tbsp Spanish olive oil
25 g/1 oz white bread
100 g/3^1/$_2$ oz blanched almonds
2 garlic cloves, crushed
pinch of saffron strands
150 ml/5 fl oz dry Spanish
    sherry or white wine
salt and pepper
300 ml/10 fl oz vegetable stock
450 g/1 lb calves' liver
plain flour, for dusting
chopped fresh flat-leaf parsley,
    to garnish
crusty bread, to serve

lamb skewers
with lemon

SERVES 8
as part of a tapas meal

2 garlic cloves, finely chopped
1 Spanish onion, finely chopped
2 tsp finely grated lemon rind
2 tbsp lemon juice
1 tsp fresh thyme leaves
1 tsp ground coriander
1 tsp ground cumin
2 tbsp red wine vinegar
125 ml/4 fl oz Spanish olive oil
1 kg/2 lb 4 oz lamb fillet,
    cut into 2-cm/³/₄-inch pieces
orange or lemon slices,
    to garnish

Mix the garlic, onion, lemon rind, lemon juice, thyme, coriander, cumin, vinegar and olive oil together in a large, shallow, non-metallic dish, whisking well until thoroughly combined.

Thread the pieces of lamb onto 16 wooden skewers and add to the dish, turning well to coat. Cover with clingfilm and leave to marinate in the refrigerator for 2–8 hours, turning occasionally.

Preheat the grill to medium. Drain the skewers, reserving the marinade. Cook under the hot grill, turning frequently and brushing with the marinade, for 10 minutes, or until tender and cooked to your liking.

Serve immediately, garnished with orange or lemon slices.

tiny meatballs
in almond sauce

SERVES 6–8
as part of a tapas meal

55 g/2 oz white or brown bread,
   crusts removed
3 tbsp water
450 g/1 lb fresh lean pork, beef
   or lamb mince
1 large onion, finely chopped
1 garlic clove, crushed
2 tbsp chopped fresh flat-leaf
   parsley, plus extra to garnish
1 egg, beaten
freshly grated nutmeg
salt and pepper
plain flour, for coating
2 tbsp Spanish olive oil
lemon juice, to taste
crusty bread, to serve

for the almond sauce
2 tbsp Spanish olive oil
25 g/1 oz white or brown bread
115 g/4 oz blanched almonds
2 garlic cloves, finely chopped
150 ml/5 fl oz dry white wine
salt and pepper
425 ml/15 fl oz vegetable stock

To prepare the meatballs, place the bread in a bowl, add the water and leave to soak for 5 minutes. With your hands, squeeze out the water and return the bread to a dry bowl. Add the pork, onion, garlic, parsley and egg, then season with grated nutmeg and a little salt and pepper. Knead the ingredients well to form a smooth mixture.

Spread some flour on a plate. With floured hands, shape the meat mixture into about 30 equal-sized balls, then roll each meatball again in flour until coated.

Heat the olive oil in a large, heavy-based frying pan. Add the meatballs, in batches, and fry for 4–5 minutes, or until browned on all sides. Using a slotted spoon, remove the meatballs from the frying pan and reserve.

To make the sauce, heat the olive oil in the same frying pan in which the meatballs were fried. Break the bread into pieces, add to the pan with the almonds and fry gently, stirring frequently, until the bread and almonds are golden brown. Add the garlic and fry for a further 30 seconds, then pour in the wine and boil for 1–2 minutes. Season to taste with salt and pepper and leave to cool slightly.

Transfer the almond mixture to a food processor. Pour in the vegetable stock and process the mixture until smooth. Return the sauce to the frying pan.

Carefully add the fried meatballs to the almond sauce and simmer for 25 minutes, or until the meatballs are tender. Taste the sauce and season with salt and pepper if necessary.

Transfer the cooked meatballs and sauce to a warmed serving dish, then add a squeeze of lemon juice to taste and sprinkle with chopped parsley to garnish. Serve piping hot with crusty bread for mopping up the almond sauce.

spanish meatballs
with cracked olives

Put the bread in a bowl, add the water and leave to soak for 5 minutes. Using your hands, squeeze out as much of the water as possible from the bread and put the bread in a clean bowl.

Add the mince, 1 chopped onion, 2 crushed garlic cloves, the cumin, coriander and egg to the bread. Season to taste with salt and, using your hands, mix together well. Dust a plate or baking sheet with flour. Using floured hands, roll the mixture into 30 equal-sized, small balls, put on the plate or baking sheet and roll lightly in the flour.

Heat 2 tablespoons of the oil in a large frying pan, add the meatballs, in batches to avoid overcrowding, and cook over a medium heat, turning frequently, for 8–10 minutes until golden brown on all sides and firm. Remove with a slotted spoon and set aside.

Heat the remaining oil in the frying pan, add the remaining onion and cook, stirring occasionally, for 5 minutes, or until softened but not browned. Add the remaining garlic and cook, stirring, for 30 seconds. Add the tomatoes, sherry, paprika and sugar and season to taste with salt. Bring to the boil, then reduce the heat and simmer for 10 minutes.

Using a handheld blender, blend the tomato mixture until smooth. Alternatively, turn the tomato mixture into a food processor or blender and process until smooth. Return the sauce to the frying pan.

Carefully return the meatballs to the frying pan and add the olives. Simmer gently for 20 minutes, or until the meatballs are tender. Serve hot, with crusty bread to mop up the sauce.

SERVES 6
as part of a tapas meal

55 g/2 oz day-old bread, crusts removed
3 tbsp water
250 g/9 oz lean fresh pork mince
250 g/9 oz lean fresh lamb mince
2 small onions, finely chopped
3 garlic cloves, crushed
1 tsp ground cumin
1 tsp ground coriander
1 egg, lightly beaten
salt
plain flour, for dusting
3 tbsp Spanish olive oil
400 g/14 oz canned chopped tomatoes
5 tbsp dry sherry or red wine
pinch of hot or sweet smoked Spanish paprika
pinch of sugar
175 g/6 oz cracked green Spanish olives in extra virgin olive oil
crusty bread, to serve

spare ribs coated in paprika sauce

SERVES 6
as part of a tapas meal

Spanish olive oil, for oiling
1.25 kg/2 lb 12 oz pork spare
  ribs
100 ml/3½ fl oz dry Spanish
  sherry
5 tsp hot or sweet smoked
  Spanish paprika
2 garlic cloves, crushed
1 tbsp dried oregano
150 ml/5 fl oz water
salt

Preheat the oven to 220°C/425°F/Gas Mark 7. Oil a large roasting tin. If the butcher has not already done so, cut the sheets of spare ribs into individual ribs. If possible, cut each spare rib in half widthways. Put the spare ribs in the prepared tin, in a single layer, and roast in the preheated oven for 20 minutes.

Meanwhile, make the sauce. Put the sherry, paprika, garlic, oregano, water and salt to taste in a jug and mix together well.

Reduce the oven temperature to 180°C/350°F/Gas Mark 4. Pour off the fat from the tin, then pour the sauce over the spare ribs and turn the spare ribs to coat with the sauce on both sides. Roast for a further 45 minutes, until tender, basting the spare ribs with the sauce once halfway through the cooking time.

Pile the spare ribs into a warmed serving dish. Bring the sauce in the roasting tin to the boil on the hob, then reduce the heat and simmer until reduced by half. Pour the sauce over the spare ribs and serve hot.

miniature pork brochettes

SERVES 4–6
as part of a tapas meal

450 g/1 lb lean boneless pork
3 tbsp Spanish olive oil,
    plus extra for oiling (optional)
grated rind and juice of
    1 large lemon
2 garlic cloves, crushed
2 tbsp chopped fresh flat-leaf
    parsley, plus extra to garnish
1 tbsp ras-el-hanout spice blend
salt and pepper

The brochettes are marinated overnight, so remember to do this in advance in order that they are ready when you need them. Cut the pork into pieces about 2 cm/³/₄ inch square and put in a large, shallow, non-metallic dish that will hold the pieces in a single layer.

To prepare the marinade, place all the remaining ingredients in a bowl and mix together. Pour the marinade over the pork and toss the meat in it until well coated. Cover the dish and leave to marinate in the refrigerator for 8 hours or overnight, stirring the pork 2–3 times.

You can use wooden or metal skewers to cook the brochettes and for this recipe you will need about 12 x 15-cm/6-inch skewers. If you are using wooden ones, soak them in cold water for 30 minutes prior to using. Metal skewers simply need to be greased.

Preheat the grill, griddle or barbecue. Thread 3 marinated pork pieces onto each prepared skewer, leaving a little space between the pieces. Cook the brochettes for 10–15 minutes, or until tender and lightly charred, turning several times and basting with the remaining marinade during cooking. Serve the pork brochettes piping hot, garnished with parsley.

serrano ham croquettes

Heat the olive oil in a saucepan, add the onion and cook over a medium heat, stirring occasionally, for 5 minutes, or until softened but not browned. Add the garlic and cook, stirring, for 30 seconds. Stir in the flour and cook over a low heat, stirring constantly, for 1 minute without the mixture colouring.

Remove the saucepan from the heat and gradually stir in the milk to form a smooth sauce. Return to the heat and slowly bring to the boil, stirring constantly, until the sauce boils and thickens.

Remove the saucepan from the heat, stir in the ham and paprika and season to taste with salt. Spread the mixture in a shallow dish and leave to cool, then cover and chill in the refrigerator for at least 2 hours or overnight.

When the mixture has chilled, break the egg onto a plate and beat lightly. Spread the breadcrumbs on a separate plate. Using wet hands, form the ham mixture into 8 even-sized pieces and form each piece into a cylindrical shape. Dip the croquettes, one at a time, into the beaten egg, then roll in the breadcrumbs to coat. Put on a plate and chill in the refrigerator for at least 1 hour.

Heat enough sunflower oil for deep-frying in a deep-fat fryer to 180–190°C/350–375°F, or until a cube of bread browns in 30 seconds. Add the croquettes, in batches to avoid overcrowding, and cook for 5 minutes, or until golden brown and crisp. Remove with a slotted spoon or draining basket and drain on kitchen paper. Keep hot in a warm oven while you cook the remaining croquettes. Serve hot with aïoli.

SERVES 4
as part of a tapas meal

4 tbsp Spanish olive oil
1 small onion, finely chopped
1 garlic clove, crushed
4 tbsp plain flour
200 ml/7 fl oz milk
200 g/7 oz Serrano ham or
    cooked ham, in one piece,
    finely diced
pinch of hot or sweet smoked
    Spanish paprika
salt
1 egg
55 g/2 oz day-old white
    breadcrumbs
sunflower oil, for deep-frying
aïoli (see page 50), to serve

empanadillas with ham & goat's cheese

SERVES 16
as part of a tapas meal

1 tbsp Spanish olive oil
1 small onion, finely chopped
1 garlic clove, crushed
150 g/5¹/₂ oz soft goat's cheese
175 g/6 oz thickly sliced cooked
  ham, finely chopped
50 g/1³/₄ oz capers, chopped
¹/₂ tsp hot or sweet smoked
  Spanish paprika
salt
500 g/1 lb 2 oz ready-made puff
  pastry, thawed if frozen
plain flour, for dusting
beaten egg, for glazing

Preheat the oven to 200°C/400°F/Gas Mark 6. Dampen several large baking sheets. Heat the oil in a large frying pan, add the onion and cook over a medium heat, stirring occasionally, for 5 minutes, or until softened but not browned. Add the garlic and cook, stirring, for 30 seconds.

Put the goat's cheese in a bowl, add the ham, capers, onion mixture and paprika and mix together well. Season to taste with salt.

Thinly roll out the pastry on a lightly floured work surface. Using a plain, 8-cm/3¹/₄-inch round cutter, cut out 32 rounds, re-rolling the trimmings as necessary. Using a teaspoon, put an equal, small amount of the goat's cheese mixture in the centre of each pastry round. Dampen the edges of the pastry with a little water and fold one half over the other to form a crescent and enclose the filling. Pinch the edges together with your fingers to seal, then press with the tines of a fork to seal further. Transfer to the prepared baking sheets.

With the tip of a sharp knife, make a small slit in the top of each pastry and brush with beaten egg to glaze. Bake in the preheated oven for 15 minutes, or until risen and golden brown. Serve warm.

chorizo in red wine

SERVES 6
as part of a tapas meal

200 g/7 oz chorizo sausage
200 ml/7 fl oz Spanish red wine
2 tbsp brandy (optional)
fresh flat-leaf parsley sprigs,
   to garnish
crusty bread, to serve

Before you begin, bear in mind that this dish is best if prepared the day before you are planning to serve it. Using a fork, prick the chorizo in 3 or 4 places. Place the chorizo and wine in a large saucepan. Bring the wine to the boil, then reduce the heat, cover and simmer gently for 15–20 minutes. Transfer the chorizo and wine to a bowl or dish, cover and leave the sausage to marinate in the wine for 8 hours or overnight.

The next day, remove the chorizo from the bowl or dish and reserve the wine. Remove the outer casing from the chorizo and cut the sausage into 5-mm/¼-inch slices. Place the slices in a large, heavy-based frying pan or flameproof serving dish.

If you are adding the brandy, pour it into a small saucepan and heat gently. Pour the brandy over the chorizo slices, stand well back and set alight. When the flames have died down, shake the pan gently, add the reserved wine to the saucepan and cook over a high heat until almost all of the wine has evaporated.

Serve the chorizo in red wine piping hot, in the pan or dish in which it was cooked, sprinkled with parsley to garnish. Accompany with chunks or slices of bread to mop up the juices and provide wooden cocktail sticks to spear the pieces of chorizo.

chickpeas & chorizo

Cut the chorizo into 1-cm/¹/₂-inch dice. Heat the oil in a large, heavy-based frying pan over a medium heat. Add the onion and garlic and fry, stirring occasionally, until the onion is softened but not browned. Stir in the chorizo and fry until heated through.

 Transfer the mixture to a bowl and stir in the chickpeas and pimientos. Splash with sherry vinegar and season to taste with salt and pepper. Serve hot or at room temperature, generously sprinkled with parsley, with plenty of crusty bread.

SERVES 4–6
as part of a tapas meal

250 g/9 oz chorizo sausage in
 1 piece, outer casing removed
4 tbsp Spanish olive oil
1 onion, finely chopped
1 large garlic clove, crushed
400 g/14 oz canned chickpeas,
 drained and rinsed
6 pimientos del piquillo, drained,
 patted dry and sliced
1 tbsp sherry vinegar, or to taste
salt and pepper
finely chopped fresh parsley,
 to garnish
crusty bread slices, to serve

chorizo & mushroom kebabs

SERVES 8
as part of a tapas meal

2 tbsp Spanish olive oil
24 slices chorizo sausage, each
    about 1 cm/1/2 inch thick
    (about 100 g/31/2 oz)
24 button mushrooms, wiped
1 green pepper, grilled, peeled
    and cut into 24 squares

Heat the olive oil in a frying pan over a medium heat. Add the chorizo
and fry for 20 seconds, stirring.

Add the mushrooms and continue frying for a further 1–2 minutes until
the mushrooms begin to brown and absorb the fat in the frying pan.

Thread a green pepper square, a piece of chorizo and a mushroom on
to a wooden cocktail stick. Continue until all the ingredients are used.
Serve hot or at room temperature.

crispy chicken
& ham croquettes

SERVES 4
as part of a tapas meal

4 tbsp Spanish olive oil or
   butter
4 tbsp plain flour
200 ml/7 fl oz milk
115 g/4 oz cooked chicken,
   minced
55 g/2 oz Serrano or cooked
   ham, very finely chopped
1 tbsp chopped fresh flat-leaf
   parsley
small pinch of freshly grated
   nutmeg
salt and pepper
1 egg, beaten
55 g/2 oz day-old white
   breadcrumbs
sunflower oil, for deep-frying
aïoli (see page 50), to serve

Heat the olive oil or butter in a saucepan. Stir in the flour to form a paste and cook gently for 1 minute, stirring constantly. Remove the saucepan from the heat and gradually stir in the milk until smooth. Return to the heat and slowly bring to the boil, stirring constantly, until the mixture boils and begins to thicken.

Remove the saucepan from the heat, add the minced chicken and beat until the mixture is smooth. Add the chopped ham, parsley and nutmeg and mix well. Season the mixture to taste with salt and pepper. Spread the chicken mixture in a dish and leave for 30 minutes until cool, then cover and leave to chill for 2–3 hours or overnight. Don't be tempted to skip this stage, as chilling the croquettes helps to stop them falling apart when they are cooked.

When the chicken mixture has chilled, pour the beaten egg onto a plate and spread the breadcrumbs out on a separate plate. Divide the chicken mixture into 8 equal-sized portions. With dampened hands, form each portion into a cylindrical shape. Dip the croquettes, one at a time, in the beaten egg, then roll in the breadcrumbs to coat them. Place on a plate and leave to chill for 1 hour.

To cook, heat the sunflower oil in a deep-fat fryer to 180–190°C/ 350–375°F, or until a cube of bread browns in 30 seconds. Add the croquettes, in batches to prevent the temperature of the oil from dropping, and deep-fry for 5–10 minutes, or until golden brown and crispy. Remove with a slotted spoon and drain well on kitchen paper.

Serve the chicken and ham croquettes piping hot, accompanied by a bowl of aïoli for dipping.

sautéed chicken
with crispy garlic slices

If necessary, halve the chicken thighs and remove the bones, then cut the flesh into bite-sized pieces, leaving the skin on. Season to taste with paprika.

Heat the oil in a large frying pan or a flameproof casserole, add the garlic slices and cook over a medium heat, stirring frequently, for 1 minute until golden brown. Remove with a slotted spoon and drain on kitchen paper.

Add the chicken thighs to the pan and cook, turning occasionally, for 10 minutes, or until tender and golden brown on all sides. Add the wine and bay leaf and bring to the boil. Reduce the heat and simmer, stirring occasionally, for 10 minutes, or until most of the liquid has evaporated and the juices run clear when a skewer is inserted into the thickest part of the meat. Season to taste with salt.

Transfer the chicken to a warmed serving dish and sprinkle over the reserved garlic slices. Scatter with chopped parsley to garnish and serve with chunks of crusty bread to mop up the juices, if desired.

SERVES 8
as part of a tapas meal

8 skin-on chicken thighs,
    boned if available
hot or sweet smoked Spanish
    paprika, to taste
4 tbsp Spanish olive oil
10 garlic cloves, sliced
125 ml/4 fl oz dry white wine
1 bay leaf
salt
chopped fresh flat-leaf parsley,
    to garnish
crusty bread, to serve (optional)

chicken rolls with olives

SERVES 6–8
as part of a tapas meal

115 g/4 oz black Spanish olives
  in oil, drained and 2 tbsp oil
  reserved
140 g/5 oz butter, softened
4 tbsp chopped fresh parsley
4 skinless, boneless chicken
  breasts

Preheat the oven to 200°C/400°F/Gas Mark 6. Stone and finely chop the olives. Mix the olives, butter and parsley together in a bowl.

Place the chicken breasts between 2 sheets of clingfilm and beat gently with a meat mallet or the side of a rolling pin.

Spread the olive and herb butter over one side of each flattened chicken breast and roll up. Secure with a wooden cocktail stick or tie with clean string if necessary.

Place the chicken rolls in an ovenproof dish. Drizzle over the oil from the olive jar and bake in the preheated oven for 45–55 minutes, or until tender and the juices run clear when the chicken is pierced with the point of a sharp knife.

Transfer the chicken rolls to a chopping board and discard the cocktail sticks or string. Using a sharp knife, cut into slices, then transfer to warmed serving plates and serve.

moroccan chicken kebabs

SERVES 4
as part of a tapas meal

450 g/1 lb chicken breast fillets
3 tbsp Spanish olive oil,
   plus extra for oiling
juice of 1 lemon
2 garlic cloves, crushed
1½ tsp ground cumin
1 tsp ground coriander
1 tsp hot or sweet smoked
   Spanish paprika
¼ tsp ground cinnamon
½ tsp dried oregano
salt
chopped fresh flat-leaf parsley,
   to garnish

Cut the chicken into 2.5-cm/1-inch cubes and put in a large, shallow, non-metallic dish. Put all the remaining ingredients, except the parsley, in a bowl and whisk together. Pour the marinade over the chicken cubes and toss the meat in the marinade until well coated. Cover and leave to marinate in the refrigerator for 8 hours or overnight, turning the chicken 2–3 times if possible.

If using wooden skewers or cocktail sticks, soak the skewers in cold water for about 30 minutes to help prevent them from burning and the food from sticking to them during cooking. If using metal skewers, lightly brush with oil. Preheat the grill, griddle or barbecue. Remove the chicken pieces from the marinade, reserving the remaining marinade, and thread an equal quantity onto each prepared skewer or cocktail stick, leaving a little space between each piece.

Brush the grill rack or griddle with a little oil, add the kebabs and cook, turning frequently and brushing with the reserved marinade halfway through cooking, for 15 minutes, or until browned on all sides, tender and cooked through. Serve hot, sprinkled with chopped parsley to garnish.

chicken wings with tomato dressing

Preheat the oven to 180°C/350°F/Gas Mark 4. Mix 1 tablespoon of the oil with the garlic and cumin in a shallow dish. Cut off and discard the tips of the chicken wings and add the wings to the spice mixture, turning to coat. Cover with clingfilm and leave to marinate in a cool place for 15 minutes.

Heat 3 tablespoons of the remaining oil in a large, heavy-based frying pan. Add the chicken wings, in batches, and cook, turning frequently, until golden brown. Transfer to a roasting tin.

Roast the chicken wings for 10–15 minutes, or until tender and the juices run clear when the point of a sharp knife is inserted into the thickest part of the meat.

Meanwhile, mix the remaining olive oil, the tomatoes, vinegar and basil together in a bowl.

Using tongs, transfer the chicken wings to a non-metallic dish. Pour the dressing over them, turning to coat. Cover with clingfilm, leave to cool, then chill for 4 hours. Remove from the refrigerator 30–60 minutes before serving to return them to room temperature.

SERVES 6–8
as part of a tapas meal

175 ml/6 fl oz Spanish olive oil
3 garlic cloves, finely chopped
1 tsp ground cumin
1 kg/2 lb 4 oz chicken wings
2 tomatoes, peeled, deseeded
  and diced
5 tbsp white wine vinegar
1 tbsp shredded fresh basil
  leaves

chicken livers
in sherry sauce

SERVES 6
as part of a tapas meal

450 g/1 lb chicken livers
2 tbsp Spanish olive oil
1 small onion, finely chopped
2 garlic cloves, finely chopped
100 ml/3½ fl oz dry Spanish
   sherry
salt and pepper
2 tbsp chopped fresh flat-leaf
   parsley, plus extra sprigs,
   to garnish
crusty bread or toast,
   to serve

If necessary, trim the chicken livers, cutting away any ducts and gristle, then cut them into small, bite-sized pieces. Heat the olive oil in a large, heavy-based frying pan. Add the onion and fry for 5 minutes, or until softened but not browned. Add the garlic and fry for a further 30 seconds.

Add the chicken livers to the pan and fry for 2–3 minutes, stirring constantly, until they are firm and have changed colour on the outside but are still pink and soft in the centre. Using a slotted spoon, lift the chicken livers from the pan, transfer them to a large, warmed serving dish or several smaller ones and keep warm.

Add the sherry to the frying pan, increase the heat and let it bubble for 3–4 minutes to evaporate the alcohol and reduce slightly. At the same time, deglaze the pan by scraping all the bits on the base of the pan into the sauce with a wooden spoon. Season the sauce to taste with salt and pepper.

Pour the sherry sauce over the chicken livers and sprinkle over the parsley. Garnish with parsley sprigs and serve piping hot with chunks or slices of crusty bread or toast to mop up the sauce.

chicken salad
with raisins & pine kernels

SERVES 6–8
as part of a tapas meal

50 ml/2 fl oz red wine vinegar
25 g/1 oz caster sugar
1 bay leaf
pared rind of 1 lemon
150 g/5½ oz seedless raisins
4 large skinless, boneless
  chicken breasts, about
  600 g/1 lb 5 oz in total
5 tbsp Spanish olive oil
1 garlic clove, finely chopped
150 g/5½ oz pine kernels
salt and pepper
100 ml/3½ fl oz Spanish
  extra virgin olive oil
1 small bunch fresh flat-leaf
  parsley, finely chopped

To make the dressing, put the vinegar, sugar, bay leaf and lemon rind in a saucepan and bring to the boil, then remove from the heat. Stir in the raisins and leave to cool.

When the dressing is cool, slice the chicken breasts widthways into very thin slices. Heat the olive oil in a large frying pan, add the chicken slices and cook over a medium heat, stirring occasionally, for 8–10 minutes until lightly browned and tender.

Add the garlic and pine kernels and cook, stirring constantly and shaking the pan, for 1 minute, or until the pine kernels are golden brown. Season to taste with salt and pepper.

Pour the cooled dressing into a large bowl, discarding the bay leaf and lemon rind. Add the extra virgin olive oil and whisk together. Season to taste with salt and pepper. Add the chicken mixture and parsley and toss together. Turn the salad into a serving dish and serve warm or, if serving cold, cover and chill in the refrigerator for 2–3 hours before serving.

fish & seafood

With miles of coastline along the Atlantic Ocean and Mediterranean, Spanish fishermen provide cooks with a wealth of fresh fish and shellfish, which results in wonderful seafood tapas, sometimes as simple as peeled prawns on cocktail sticks.

Yet even with such fresh choices, Spaniards retain a soft spot for salt cod, often the only seafood available in the days before modern transportation, and Salt Cod Fritters with Spinach are always popular.

This chapter contains recipes from all over the country, and land and sea come together in Scallops with Serrano Ham and Rosemary Skewers with Monkfish & Bacon. In the sunny south, Sizzling Chilli Prawns is the ubiquitous tapas.

salt cod fritters
with spinach

SERVES 16
as part of a tapas meal

250 g/9 oz dried salt cod in
   1 piece
140 g/5 oz plain flour
1 tsp baking powder
1/4 tsp salt
1 large egg, lightly beaten
about 150 ml/5 fl oz milk
2 lemon slices
2 fresh parsley sprigs
1 bay leaf
1/2 tbsp garlic-flavoured olive oil
85 g/3 oz fresh baby spinach,
   rinsed
1/4 tsp smoked sweet, mild or
   hot Spanish paprika, to taste
Spanish olive oil, for frying
coarse sea salt (optional)
aïoli (see page 50), to serve

Place the dried salt cod in a large bowl, cover with cold water and leave to soak for 48 hours, changing the water at least 3 times a day.

When the cod is prepared and ready to use, make the batter. Sift the flour, baking powder and salt into a large bowl and make a well. Mix the egg with 100 ml/3 1/2 fl oz of the milk and pour into the well in the flour, stirring to make a smooth batter with a thick coating consistency. If it seems too thick, gradually stir in the remaining milk, then leave to stand for at least 1 hour.

After the salt cod has soaked, transfer it to a large frying pan. Add the lemon slices, parsley sprigs, bay leaf and enough water to cover and bring to the boil. Reduce the heat and simmer for 30–45 minutes until the fish is tender and flakes easily.

Meanwhile, prepare the spinach. Heat the garlic-flavoured olive oil in a small saucepan over a medium heat. Add the spinach with just the water clinging to the leaves and cook for 3–4 minutes until wilted.

Drain the spinach in a sieve, using the back of a spoon to press out any excess moisture. Finely chop the spinach, then stir it into the batter with the paprika.

Remove the fish from the water and flake the flesh into pieces, removing all the skin and tiny bones. Stir the flesh into the batter.

Heat 5-cm/2-inch of olive oil in a heavy-based frying pan to 180–190°C/350–375°F, or until a cube of bread browns in 30 seconds. Use a greased tablespoon or measuring spoon to drop spoonfuls of the batter into the oil and fry for 8–10 minutes until golden brown. Work in batches to avoid crowding the pan. Use a slotted spoon to transfer the fritters to kitchen paper to drain and sprinkle with sea salt, if using.

Serve hot or at room temperature with aïoli for dipping.

sardines with romesco sauce

SERVES 6
as part of a tapas meal

24 fresh sardines, scaled,
    cleaned and heads removed
115 g/4 oz plain flour
4 eggs, lightly beaten
250 g/9 oz fresh white
    breadcrumbs
6 tbsp chopped fresh parsley
4 tbsp chopped fresh marjoram
vegetable oil, for deep-frying

for the romesco sauce
1 red pepper, halved and
    deseeded
2 tomatoes, halved
4 garlic cloves
125 ml/4 fl oz Spanish olive oil
1 slice white bread, diced
4 tbsp blanched almonds
1 fresh red chilli, deseeded and
    chopped
2 shallots, chopped
1 tsp paprika
2 tbsp red wine vinegar
2 tsp sugar
1 tbsp water

First make the sauce. Preheat the oven to 220°C/425°F/Gas Mark 7. Place the pepper, tomatoes and garlic in an ovenproof dish and drizzle over 1 tablespoon of the olive oil, turning to coat. Bake in the preheated oven for 20–25 minutes, then remove from the oven and cool. Peel off the skins and place the flesh in a food processor.

Heat 1 tablespoon of the remaining oil in a frying pan. Add the bread and almonds and cook over a low heat for a few minutes, or until browned. Remove and drain on kitchen paper. Add the chilli, shallots and paprika to the pan and cook for a further 5 minutes, or until the shallots are softened.

Transfer the almond mixture and shallot mixture to a food processor and add the vinegar, sugar and water. Process to a paste. With the motor still running, gradually add the remaining oil through the feeder tube. Transfer to a bowl, cover and reserve.

Place the sardines, skin-side up, on a chopping board and press along the length of the spines with your thumbs. Turn over and remove and discard the bones. Place the flour and eggs in separate bowls. Mix the breadcrumbs and herbs together in a third bowl. Toss the fish in the flour, the eggs, then in the breadcrumbs.

Heat the vegetable oil in a large saucepan to 180–190°C/350–375°F, or until a cube of bread browns in 30 seconds. Deep-fry the fish for 4–5 minutes, or until golden and tender. Drain and serve with the sauce.

fresh salmon with red pepper sauce

Preheat the oven to 200°C/400°F/Gas Mark 6. Brush the red peppers with 2 teaspoons of the oil and put in a roasting tin. Roast in the preheated oven for 30 minutes, turn over and roast for a further 10 minutes until the skins have blistered and blackened.

Meanwhile, remove the skin from the salmon fillets and cut the flesh into 2.5-cm/1-inch cubes. Season to taste with pepper and set aside.

Heat 2 tablespoons of the remaining oil in a large frying pan, add the onion and cook, stirring occasionally, for 5 minutes, or until softened but not browned. Add the garlic and cook, stirring, for 30 seconds until softened. Add the wine, bring to the boil and leave to bubble for 1 minute. Remove from the heat and set aside.

When the peppers are cooked, transfer to a polythene bag using a slotted spoon and leave for 15 minutes, or until cool enough to handle. Using a sharp knife or your fingers, carefully peel away the skin from the peppers. Halve the peppers and remove the stems, cores and seeds, then put the flesh in a food processor.

Add the onion mixture and cream to the peppers and process to a smooth purée. Season to taste with salt and pepper. Pour into a saucepan.

Heat the remaining oil in the frying pan, add the salmon cubes and cook, turning occasionally, for 8–10 minutes until cooked through and golden brown on both sides. Meanwhile, gently heat the sauce in the saucepan.

Transfer the cooked salmon to a warmed serving dish, drizzle over some of the pepper sauce and serve the remaining sauce in a small serving bowl. Serve hot, garnished with chopped parsley and accompanied by crusty bread to mop up the sauce, if desired.

SERVES 6
as part of a tapas meal

2 red peppers
about 4 tbsp Spanish olive oil
700 g/1 lb 9 oz salmon fillets
salt and pepper
1 onion, roughly chopped
1 garlic clove, finely chopped
6 tbsp dry white wine
100 ml/3 1/2 fl oz double cream
chopped fresh flat-leaf parsley,
  to garnish
crusty bread, to serve (optional)

rosemary skewers
with monkfish & bacon

SERVES 12
as part of a tapas meal

350 g/12 oz monkfish tail or
   250 g/9 oz monkfish fillet
12 fresh rosemary stalks
3 tbsp Spanish olive oil
juice of 1/2 small lemon
1 garlic clove, crushed
salt and pepper
6 thick back bacon rashers
lemon wedges, to garnish
aïoli (see page 50), to serve

If using monkfish tail, cut either side of the central bone with a sharp knife and remove the flesh to form 2 fillets. Slice the fillets in half lengthways, then cut each fillet into 12 bite-sized chunks to give a total of 24 pieces. Place the monkfish pieces in a large bowl.

To prepare the rosemary skewers, strip the leaves off the stalks and reserve them, leaving a few leaves at one end. For the marinade, finely chop the reserved leaves and whisk together in a bowl with the olive oil, lemon juice, garlic and salt and pepper to taste. Add the monkfish pieces and toss until coated in the marinade. Cover and leave to marinate in the refrigerator for 1–2 hours.

Cut each bacon rasher in half lengthways, then in half widthways, and roll up each piece. Thread 2 pieces of monkfish alternately with 2 bacon rolls onto each of the prepared rosemary skewers.

Preheat the grill, griddle or barbecue. Grill the monkfish and bacon skewers for 10 minutes, turning occasionally and basting with any remaining marinade, or until cooked. Serve hot, garnished with lemon wedges for squeezing over the monkfish skewers and accompanied by a small bowl of aïoli in which to dip them.

mixed seafood kebabs
with a chilli & lime glaze

SERVES 4
as part of a tapas meal

16 raw tiger prawns, in their
    shells
350 g/12 oz monkfish or hake
    fillet
350 g/12 oz salmon fillet,
    skinned
2.5-cm/1-inch piece fresh
    root ginger
4 tbsp sweet chilli sauce
grated rind and juice of 1 lime
sunflower or Spanish olive oil,
    for oiling (optional)
lime wedges, to serve

Pull off the heads of the prawns. With your fingers, peel away the shells, leaving the tails intact. Using a sharp knife, make a shallow slit along the length of the back of each prawn, then use the tip of the knife to lift out the dark vein and discard. Rinse the prawns under cold running water and pat dry with kitchen paper. Cut the monkfish and salmon into 2.5-cm/ 1-inch pieces.

Grate the ginger into a sieve set over a large, non-metallic bowl to catch the juice. Squeeze the grated ginger to extract all the juice and discard the pulp.

Add the chilli sauce and lime rind and juice to the ginger juice and mix together. Add the prepared seafood and stir to coat in the marinade. Cover and leave to marinate in the refrigerator for 30 minutes.

Meanwhile, if using wooden skewers, soak 8 in cold water for about 30 minutes to help prevent them from burning and the food sticking to them during cooking. If using metal skewers, lightly brush with oil.

Preheat the grill to high and line the grill pan with foil. Remove the seafood from the marinade, reserving the remaining marinade, and thread an equal quantity onto each prepared skewer, leaving a little space between each piece. Arrange in the grill pan.

Cook the skewers under the grill, turning once and brushing with the reserved marinade, for 6–8 minutes until cooked through. Serve hot, drizzled with the marinade in the grill pan and with lime wedges for squeezing over.

batter-fried fish sticks

To make the batter, put the flour and salt into a large bowl and make a well in the centre. Pour the egg and olive oil into the well, then gradually add the water, mixing in the flour from the side and beating constantly, until all the flour is incorporated and a smooth batter forms.

Cut the fish into sticks about 2 cm/³/₄ inch wide and 5 cm/2 inches long. Dust lightly with flour so that the batter sticks to them when they are dipped in it.

Heat enough sunflower or olive oil for deep-frying in a deep-fat fryer to 180–190°C/350–375°F, or until a cube of bread browns in 30 seconds. Spear a fish stick onto a cocktail stick, dip into the batter and then drop the fish and cocktail stick into the hot oil. Cook the fish sticks, in batches to avoid overcrowding, for 5 minutes, or until golden brown. Remove with a slotted spoon or draining basket and drain on kitchen paper. Keep hot in a warm oven while cooking the remaining fish sticks.

Serve the fish sticks hot, with lemon wedges for squeezing over.

SERVES 6
as part of a tapas meal

115 g/4 oz plain flour, plus extra for dusting
pinch of salt
1 egg, beaten
1 tbsp Spanish olive oil
150 ml/5 fl oz water
600 g/1 lb 5 oz firm-fleshed white fish fillet, such as monkfish or hake
sunflower or Spanish olive oil, for deep-frying
lemon wedges, to serve

tuna-stuffed pepper strips

SERVES 8
as part of a tapas meal

6 mixed red, green, yellow or
   orange peppers
2 tbsp Spanish olive oil
200 g/7 oz canned tuna in olive
   oil, drained
100 g/3½ oz curd cheese
4 tbsp chopped fresh flat-leaf
   parsley
1 garlic clove, crushed
salt and pepper

Preheat the oven to 200°C/400°F/Gas Mark 6. Brush the peppers with the oil and put in a roasting tin. Roast in the preheated oven for 30 minutes, turn over and roast for a further 10 minutes until the skins have blistered and blackened.

Using a slotted spoon, transfer the roasted peppers to a polythene bag and leave to cool for about 15 minutes, or until cool enough to handle.

Meanwhile, put the tuna on kitchen paper and pat dry to remove the oil. Transfer to a food processor, add the curd cheese, parsley and garlic and process until mixed together. Season to taste with salt and pepper. Using a sharp knife or your fingers, carefully peel away the skins from the cooled peppers. Cut the peppers into quarters and remove the stems, cores and seeds.

Put a heaped teaspoonful of the tuna and cheese mixture on the pointed end of each pepper quarter and roll up. If necessary, wipe with kitchen paper to remove any filling that has spread over the outsides of the rolls, then arrange the rolls in a shallow dish with the filling end facing up. Cover and chill in the refrigerator for at least 2 hours until firm before serving.

empanadillas with tuna & olives

SERVES 16
as part of a tapas meal

175 g/6 oz canned tuna in
   olive oil
1 small onion, finely chopped
1 garlic clove, finely chopped
50 g/1¾ oz pimiento-stuffed
   Spanish olives, finely chopped
25 g/1 oz pine kernels
salt and pepper
500 g/1 lb 2 oz ready-made puff
   pastry, thawed if frozen
plain flour, for dusting
beaten egg, for glazing

Drain the tuna, reserving the oil, put in a large bowl and set aside. Heat
1 tablespoon of the reserved oil from the tuna in a large frying pan,
add the onion and cook over a medium heat, stirring occasionally, for
5 minutes, or until softened but not browned. Add the garlic and cook,
stirring, for 30 seconds until softened.

Mash the tuna with a fork, then add the onion mixture, olives and pine
kernels and mix together well. Season to taste with salt and pepper.

Preheat the oven to 200°C/400°F/Gas Mark 6. Dampen several large
baking sheets. Thinly roll out the pastry on a lightly floured work surface.
Using a plain, 8-cm/3¼-inch round cutter, cut out 32 rounds, re-rolling
the trimmings as necessary. Using a teaspoon, put an equal, small amount
of the tuna mixture in the centre of each pastry round. Dampen the
edges of the pastry with a little water and fold one half over the other
to form a crescent and enclose the filling. Pinch the edges together with
your fingers to seal, then press with the tines of a fork to seal further.
Transfer to the prepared baking sheets.

With the tip of a sharp knife, make a small slit in the top of each pastry
and brush with beaten egg to glaze. Bake in the preheated oven for
15 minutes, or until risen and golden brown. Serve warm.

seared squid & golden potatoes

Put the potatoes in a saucepan of water and bring to the boil. Reduce the heat and simmer for 20 minutes, or until tender. Drain well.

Heat 4 tablespoons of oil in a large flameproof casserole, add the potatoes and cook over a medium heat, stirring occasionally, for 10 minutes, or until beginning to turn brown. Add the onion and cook, stirring occasionally, for 10 minutes until golden brown. Add the garlic and cook, stirring, for 30 seconds until softened. Push all the ingredients to the side of the casserole.

If necessary, add the remaining oil to the casserole. Add the squid slices and cook over a high heat, stirring occasionally, for 2 minutes, or until golden brown. Add the wine and cook for a further 1–2 minutes. Add most of the parsley, reserving a little to garnish, and mix the potatoes, onions and garlic with the squid. Season to taste with salt and pepper.

Serve hot, in the casserole, sprinkled with the reserved parsley to garnish and with lemon wedges for squeezing over.

SERVES 8
as part of a tapas meal

1 kg/2 lb 4 oz new potatoes
4–6 tbsp Spanish olive oil
1 large onion, thinly sliced
2 garlic cloves, finely chopped
1 kg/2 lb 4 oz cleaned squid
   bodies, thinly sliced
6 tbsp dry white wine
1 small bunch fresh flat-leaf
   parsley, finely chopped
salt and pepper
lemon wedges, to serve

calamari with prawns & broad beans

SERVES 4–6
as part of a tapas meal

2 tbsp Spanish olive oil
4 spring onions, thinly sliced
2 garlic cloves, finely chopped
500 g/1 lb 2 oz cleaned squid
  bodies, thickly sliced
100 ml/3½ fl oz dry white wine
600 g/1 lb 5 oz fresh young
  broad beans in their pods,
  shelled to give about 225 g/
  8 oz, or 225 g/8 oz frozen
  baby broad beans
250 g/9 oz raw tiger prawns,
  peeled and deveined
4 tbsp chopped fresh flat-leaf
  parsley
salt and pepper
crusty bread, to serve

Heat the oil in a large frying pan with a lid or a flameproof casserole, add the spring onions and cook over a medium heat, stirring occasionally, for 4–5 minutes until softened. Add the garlic and cook, stirring, for 30 seconds until softened. Add the squid slices and cook over a high heat, stirring occasionally, for 2 minutes, or until golden brown.

Add the wine and bring to the boil. Add the broad beans, then reduce the heat, cover and simmer for 5–8 minutes if using fresh beans or 4–5 minutes if using frozen beans until the beans are tender.

Add the prawns and parsley, re-cover and simmer for a further 2–3 minutes until the prawns turn pink and start to curl. Season to taste with salt and pepper. Serve hot, with crusty bread to mop up the juices.

tossed prawns with peppers

SERVES 8
as part of a tapas meal

500 g/1 lb 2 oz raw tiger
   prawns, in their shells
2 tbsp Spanish olive oil
2 red peppers, cored, deseeded
   and thinly sliced
5 garlic cloves, finely chopped
juice of 1/2 lemon
6 tbsp dry Spanish sherry
salt and pepper
crusty bread, to serve

Pull off the heads of the prawns. With your fingers, peel away the shells, leaving the tails intact. Using a sharp knife, make a shallow slit along the length of the back of each prawn, then use the tip of the knife to lift out the dark vein and discard. Rinse the prawns under cold running water and pat dry with kitchen paper.

Heat the oil in a large frying pan, add the red pepper slices and cook for 10–15 minutes until softened. Add the garlic and cook, stirring, for 30 seconds until softened. Add the prawns to the frying pan and cook, tossing constantly, for 1–2 minutes until the prawns turn pink. Add the lemon juice and sherry and cook for a further 2 minutes until the prawns begin to curl. Season to taste with salt and pepper.

Serve hot, with chunks or slices of crusty bread to mop up the juices.

sizzling chilli prawns

Pull the heads off the prawns and peel, leaving the tails intact. Cut along the length of the back of each prawn and remove and discard the dark vein. Rinse the prawns under cold running water and pat dry on kitchen paper.

Cut the chilli in half lengthways, remove the seeds and finely chop the flesh.

Heat the olive oil in a large, heavy-based frying pan or flameproof casserole until quite hot, then add the garlic and fry for 30 seconds. Add the prawns, chilli, paprika and a pinch of salt and fry for 2–3 minutes, stirring constantly, until the prawns turn pink and begin to curl.

Serve the prawns in the cooking dish, still sizzling. Accompany with wooden cocktail sticks, to spear the prawns, and chunks or slices of crusty bread to mop up the aromatic cooking oil.

SERVES 6
as part of a tapas meal

500 g/1 lb 2 oz raw tiger
    prawns, in their shells
1 small fresh red chilli
6 tbsp Spanish olive oil
2 garlic cloves, finely chopped
pinch of paprika
salt
crusty bread, to serve

saffron prawns with lemon mayonnaise

SERVES 6–8
as part of a tapas meal

1.25 kg/2 lb 12 oz raw jumbo
    prawns
85 g/3 oz plain flour
125 ml/4 fl oz light beer
2 tbsp Spanish olive oil
pinch of saffron powder
2 egg whites
vegetable oil, for deep-frying

for the lemon mayonnaise
4 garlic cloves
sea salt and pepper
2 egg yolks
1 tbsp lemon juice
1 tbsp finely grated lemon rind
300 ml/10 fl oz sunflower oil

First make the mayonnaise. Place the garlic cloves on a chopping board and sprinkle with a little sea salt, then flatten them with the side of a heavy knife. Finely chop and flatten again.

Transfer the garlic to a food processor or blender and add the egg yolks, lemon juice and lemon rind. Process briefly until just blended. With the motor still running, gradually add the sunflower oil through the feeder tube until it is fully incorporated. Scrape the mayonnaise into a serving bowl, season to taste with salt and pepper, then cover and leave to chill until ready to serve.

Pull the heads off the prawns and peel, leaving the tails intact. Cut along the length of the back of each prawn and remove and discard the dark vein. Rinse under cold running water and pat dry with kitchen paper.

Sift the flour into a bowl. Mix the beer, oil and saffron together in a jug, then gradually whisk into the flour. Cover and leave at room temperature for 30 minutes to rest.

Whisk the egg whites in a spotlessly clean, greasefree bowl until stiff. Gently fold the egg whites into the flour mixture.

Heat the vegetable oil in a deep-fat fryer or large saucepan to 180–190°C/350–375°F, or until a cube of bread browns in 30 seconds. Holding the prawns by their tails, dip them into the batter and shake off any excess. Add the prawns to the oil and deep-fry for 2–3 minutes, or until crisp. Remove with a slotted spoon and drain well on kitchen paper. Serve immediately with the mayonnaise.

crab tartlets

SERVES 12
as part of a tapas meal

1 tbsp Spanish olive oil
1 small onion, finely chopped
1 garlic clove, finely chopped
splash of dry white wine
2 eggs
150 ml/5 fl oz milk or single
    cream
175 g/6 oz canned crabmeat,
    drained
55 g/2 oz Manchego or
    Parmesan cheese, grated
2 tbsp chopped fresh flat-leaf
    parsley
pinch of freshly grated nutmeg
salt and pepper
fresh dill sprigs, to garnish

for the pastry
350 g/12 oz plain flour,
    plus extra for dusting
pinch of salt
175 g/6 oz butter
2 tbsp cold water

or
500 g/1 lb 2 oz ready-made
    shortcrust pastry

Preheat the oven to 190°C/375°F/Gas Mark 5. To prepare the crabmeat filling, heat the olive oil in a saucepan. Add the onion and fry for 5 minutes, or until softened but not browned. Add the garlic and fry for a further 30 seconds. Add a splash of white wine and cook for 1–2 minutes, or until most of the wine has evaporated.

Lightly whisk the eggs in a large bowl, then whisk in the milk or cream. Add the crabmeat, grated cheese, parsley and the onion mixture. Season the mixture with nutmeg and salt and pepper to taste and mix together.

To prepare the pastry if you are making it yourself, mix the flour and salt together in a large bowl. Add the butter, cut into small pieces, and rub it in until the mixture resembles fine breadcrumbs. Gradually stir in enough of the water to form a firm dough. Alternatively, the pastry could be made in a food processor.

Thinly roll out the pastry on a lightly floured work surface. Using a plain, round 7-cm/2³/4-inch cutter, cut the pastry into 18 rounds. Gently pile the trimmings together, roll out again, then cut out a further 6 rounds. Use to line 24 x 4-cm/1¹/2-inch tartlet tins. Carefully spoon the crabmeat mixture into the pastry cases, taking care not to overfill them.

Bake the tartlets in the preheated oven for 25–30 minutes, or until golden brown and set. Serve the crab tartlets hot or cold, garnished with fresh dill sprigs.

sweet peppers stuffed with crab salad

First make the crab salad. Pick over the crabmeat and remove any bits of shell. Put half the crabmeat in a food processor with the prepared red pepper, 1 1/2 tablespoons of the lemon juice and salt and pepper to taste. Process until well blended, then transfer to a bowl. Stir in the cream cheese and remaining crabmeat. Taste and add extra lemon juice, if required.

Pat the pimientos del piquillo dry and scoop out any seeds that remain in the tips. Use a small spoon to divide the crab salad equally among the peppers, stuffing them generously. Arrange on a large serving dish or individual plates, cover and leave to chill until ready to serve. Just before serving, sprinkle the stuffed peppers with the chopped parsley.

SERVES 8
as part of a tapas meal

16 pimientos del piquillo,
    drained, or freshly roasted
    peppers, tops cut off
chopped fresh parsley,
    to garnish

for the crab salad
240 g/8 1/2 oz canned crabmeat,
    drained and squeezed dry
1 red pepper, grilled, peeled
    and chopped
about 2 tbsp fresh lemon juice
salt and pepper
200 g/7 oz cream cheese

scallops with serrano ham

SERVES 4
as part of a tapas meal

2 tbsp lemon juice
3 tbsp Spanish olive oil
2 garlic cloves, finely chopped
1 tbsp chopped fresh parsley
12 shelled scallops, preferably
  with corals
8 wafer-thin slices Serrano
  ham
pepper

Mix the lemon juice, olive oil, garlic and parsley together in a non-metallic dish. Separate the corals, if using, from the scallops and add both to the dish, turning to coat. Cover with clingfilm and leave to marinate at room temperature for 20 minutes.

Preheat the grill to medium. Drain the scallops, reserving the marinade. Thread a scallop and a coral, if using, onto a metal skewer. Scrunch up a slice of ham and thread onto the skewer, followed by another scallop and a coral. Repeat to fill 4 skewers, each with 3 scallops and 2 slices of ham.

Cook under the hot grill, basting generously with the marinade and turning frequently, for 5 minutes, or until the scallops are tender and the ham is crisp.

Transfer to warmed serving plates, sprinkle them with pepper, spoon over the cooking juices from the grill pan and serve.

mussels in a vinaigrette dressing

SERVES 6
as part of a tapas meal

6 tbsp Spanish extra virgin
   olive oil
2 tbsp white wine vinegar
1 shallot, finely chopped
1 garlic clove, crushed
2 tbsp capers, chopped
1 fresh red chilli, deseeded and
   finely chopped (optional)
salt and pepper
1 kg/2 lb 4 oz live mussels,
   in their shells
6 tbsp dry white wine
4 tbsp chopped fresh
   flat-leaf parsley
crusty bread, to serve (optional)

To make the dressing, put the oil and vinegar in a bowl and whisk together. Stir in the shallot, garlic, capers and chilli, if using. Season to taste with salt and pepper.

Clean the mussels by scrubbing or scraping the shells and pulling out any beards that are attached to them. Discard any with broken shells or any that refuse to close when tapped. Put the mussels in a colander and rinse well under cold running water.

Put the mussels in a large saucepan and add the wine. Bring to the boil, cover and cook over a high heat, shaking the pan occasionally, for 3–4 minutes, or until the mussels have opened. Drain the mussels, discarding any that remain closed, and leave to cool.

When the mussels are cool enough to handle, discard the empty half-shells and arrange the mussels, in their other half-shells, in a large, shallow serving dish. Whisk the dressing again and spoon over the mussels. Cover and chill in the refrigerator for at least 1 hour.

To serve, sprinkle the parsley over the top and serve with crusty bread to mop up the dressing, if desired.

mussels with garlic butter

Clean the mussels by scrubbing or scraping the shells and pulling out any beards that are attached to them. Discard any with broken shells and any that refuse to close when sharply tapped with the back of a knife. Place the mussels in a colander and rinse under cold running water.

Place the mussels in a large saucepan and add a splash of wine and the bay leaf. Cook, covered, over a high heat for 5 minutes, shaking the saucepan occasionally, or until the mussels are opened. Drain the mussels and discard any that remain closed.

Shell the mussels, reserving one half of each shell. Arrange the mussels, in their half-shells, in a large, shallow, ovenproof serving dish.

Melt the butter and pour into a bowl. Add the breadcrumbs, parsley, chives, garlic and salt and pepper to taste and mix well together. Leave until the butter has set slightly. Using your fingers or 2 teaspoons, take a large pinch of the herb and butter mixture and use to fill each mussel shell, pressing it down well. Leave the mussels to chill until ready to serve.

To serve, preheat the oven to 230°C/450°F/Gas Mark 8. Bake the mussels in the preheated oven for 10 minutes, or until hot. Serve immediately, garnished with parsley sprigs and accompanied by lemon wedges for squeezing over them.

SERVES 8
as part of a tapas meal

800 g/1 lb 12 oz live mussels,
    in their shells
splash of dry white wine
1 bay leaf
85 g/3 oz butter
350 g/12 oz fresh white or
    brown breadcrumbs
4 tbsp chopped fresh flat-leaf
    parsley, plus extra sprigs
    to garnish
2 tbsp snipped fresh chives
2 garlic cloves, finely chopped
salt and pepper
lemon wedges, to serve

oysters with sherry vinegar

SERVES 6
as part of a tapas meal

1 shallot, finely chopped
3 tbsp sherry vinegar
3 tbsp red wine vinegar
1 tbsp sugar
pepper
24 fresh oysters
rock salt or crushed ice,
    to serve (optional)

Mix the shallot, vinegars and sugar together in a non-metallic bowl and season well with pepper. Cover with clingfilm and leave to stand at room temperature for at least 15 minutes to allow the flavours to mingle.

Meanwhile, shuck the oysters. Wrap a tea towel around your hand to protect it and hold an oyster firmly. Insert an oyster knife or other strong, sharp knife into the hinged edge and twist to prise the shells apart. Still holding both shells firmly in the wrapped hand, slide the blade of the knife along the upper shell to sever the muscle. Lift off the upper shell, being careful not to spill the liquid inside. Slide the blade of the knife along the lower shell underneath the oyster to sever the second muscle. Arrange the oysters on their half-shells in a single layer on a bed of rock salt or crushed ice, if you like.

Spoon the dressing evenly over the oysters and serve at room temperature.

clams in tomato & garlic sauce

SERVES 6–8
as part of a tapas meal

2 hard-boiled eggs, cooled,
    shelled and halved lengthways
3 tbsp Spanish olive oil
1 Spanish onion, chopped
2 garlic cloves, finely chopped
700 g/1 lb 9 oz tomatoes,
    peeled and diced
40 g/1½ oz fresh white
    breadcrumbs
salt and pepper
1 kg/2 lb 4 oz fresh clams
425 ml/15 fl oz dry white wine
2 tbsp chopped fresh parsley
lemon wedges, to garnish

Scoop out the egg yolks using a teaspoon and rub through a fine sieve into a bowl. Chop the whites and reserve separately.

Heat the olive oil in a large, heavy-based frying pan. Add the onion and cook over a low heat, stirring occasionally, for 5 minutes, or until softened. Add the garlic and cook for a further 3 minutes, then add the tomatoes, breadcrumbs and egg yolks and season to taste with salt and pepper. Cook, stirring occasionally and mashing the mixture with a wooden spoon, for a further 10–15 minutes, or until thick and pulpy.

Meanwhile, scrub the clams under cold running water. Discard any with broken shells or any that do not close immediately when sharply tapped with the back of a knife.

Place the clams in a large, heavy-based saucepan. Add the wine and bring to the boil. Cover and cook over a high heat, shaking the saucepan occasionally, for 3–5 minutes, or until the clams have opened. Discard any that remain closed.

Using a slotted spoon, transfer the clams to warmed serving bowls. Strain the cooking liquid into the tomato sauce, stir well and spoon over the clams. Sprinkle with the chopped egg whites and parsley and serve immediately, garnished with lemon wedges.

eggs & cheese

Eggs and cheese are two essential ingredients in Spanish cooking, offering

great scope for many inexpensive tapas recipes. Nothing symbolizes the

essence of tapas more than the thick egg and potato omelette called Spanish

Tortilla. Made with such humble ingredients and once a meagre meal for poor

labourers, it is now the nation's favourite tapas. This chapter contains many

satisfying variations, but whichever you try, it will be delicious hot or at room

temperature. Oven-baked Tortilla, cut into tiny squares and speared on

cocktail sticks, makes a good party dish. Cheese Puffs with Fiery Tomato Salsa

are perennially popular, while Figs with Blue Cheese make good use of

wonderfully fresh ingredients.

spanish tortilla

SERVES 8
as part of a tapas meal

125 ml/4 fl oz Spanish olive oil
600 g/1 lb 5 oz potatoes, peeled
   and thinly sliced
1 large onion, thinly sliced
6 large eggs
salt and pepper
fresh flat-leaf parsley,
   to garnish

Heat a non-stick 25-cm/10-inch frying pan over a high heat. Add the olive oil and heat. Reduce the heat, then add the potatoes and onion and cook for 15–20 minutes, or until the potatoes are tender.

Beat the eggs in a large bowl and season generously with salt and pepper. Drain the potatoes and onion through a sieve over a heatproof bowl to reserve the oil. Very gently stir the vegetables into the eggs, then leave to stand for 10 minutes.

Use a wooden spoon or spatula to remove any crusty bits stuck to the base of the frying pan. Reheat the frying pan over a medium heat with 4 tablespoons of the reserved oil. Add the egg mixture and smooth the surface, pressing the potatoes and onions into an even layer.

Cook for 5 minutes, shaking the frying pan occasionally, until the base is set. Use a spatula to loosen the side of the tortilla. Place a large plate over the top and carefully invert the frying pan and plate together so the tortilla drops onto the plate.

Add 1 tablespoon of the remaining reserved oil to the frying pan and swirl around. Carefully slide the tortilla back into the frying pan, cooked-side up. Run the spatula around the tortilla, to tuck in the edge.

Continue cooking for 3 minutes, or until the eggs are set and the base is golden brown. Remove the frying pan from the heat and slide the tortilla on to a plate. Leave to stand for at least 5 minutes before cutting. Garnish with parsley and serve.

oven-baked tortilla

SERVES 16
as part of a tapas meal

4 tbsp Spanish olive oil, plus
    extra for oiling
1 large garlic clove, crushed
4 spring onions, white and
    green parts finely chopped
1 green pepper, deseeded and
    finely diced
1 red pepper, deseeded and
    finely diced
175 g/6 oz potato, boiled,
    peeled and diced
5 large eggs
100 ml/3$\frac{1}{2}$ fl oz soured cream
175 g/6 oz Spanish Rocal,
    Cheddar or Parmesan
    cheese, grated
3 tbsp snipped fresh chives
salt and pepper
slices of bread, to serve
green salad, to serve

Preheat the oven to 190°C/375°F/Gas Mark 5. Line an 18 x 25-cm/
7 x 10-inch baking tray with foil and brush with a little olive oil. Reserve.

Place the olive oil, garlic, spring onions and peppers in a frying pan.
Cook over a medium heat, stirring, for 10 minutes, or until the onions are
softened but not browned. Leave to cool, then stir in the potato.

Beat the eggs, soured cream, cheese and chives together in a large
bowl. Stir the cooled vegetables into the bowl and season to taste with
salt and pepper.

Pour the mixture into the baking tray and smooth over the top. Bake in
the preheated oven for 30–40 minutes, or until golden brown, puffed and
set in the centre. Remove from the oven and leave to cool and set. Run
a spatula around the edge, then invert onto a chopping board, browned-
side down, and peel off the foil. If the surface looks a little runny, place it
under a medium grill to dry out.

Leave to cool completely. Trim the edges if necessary, then cut into 48
squares. Serve on a platter with wooden cocktail sticks, or secure each
square to a slice of bread, and accompany with green salad.

chorizo & broad bean tortilla

Cook the broad beans in a saucepan of boiling water for 4 minutes. Drain well and leave to cool. Meanwhile, lightly beat the eggs in a large bowl. Add the chorizo sausage and season to taste with salt and pepper.

When the beans are cool enough to handle, slip off their skins. This is a laborious task, but worth doing if you have the time. This quantity will take about 15 minutes to skin.

Heat the oil in a large frying pan, add the onion and cook over a medium heat, stirring occasionally, for 5 minutes, or until softened but not browned. Add the broad beans and cook, stirring, for 1 minute. Pour the egg mixture into the frying pan and cook gently for 2–3 minutes until the underside is just set and lightly browned. Use a spatula to loosen the tortilla away from the side and base of the frying pan to allow the uncooked egg to run underneath and prevent the tortilla from sticking to the base.

Cover the tortilla with a large, upside-down plate and invert the tortilla onto it. Slide the tortilla back into the frying pan, cooked-side up, and cook for a further 2–3 minutes until the underside is lightly browned.

Slide the tortilla onto a warmed serving dish. Serve warm, cut into small cubes.

SERVES 8
as part of a tapas meal

225 g/8 oz frozen baby
   broad beans
6 eggs
100 g/3¹/₂ oz chorizo sausage,
   outer casing removed,
   chopped
salt and pepper
3 tbsp Spanish olive oil
1 onion, chopped

spinach & mushroom tortilla

SERVES 8
as part of a tapas meal

2 tbsp Spanish olive oil
3 shallots, finely chopped
350 g/12 oz mushrooms, sliced
280 g/10 oz fresh spinach
  leaves, coarse stalks
  removed
salt and pepper
55 g/2 oz toasted flaked
  almonds
5 eggs
2 tbsp chopped fresh parsley
2 tbsp cold water
85 g/3 oz mature Mahon,
  Manchego or Parmesan
  cheese, grated

Heat the olive oil in a frying pan that can safely be placed under the grill. Add the shallots and cook over a low heat, stirring occasionally, for 5 minutes, or until softened. Add the mushrooms and cook, stirring frequently, for a further 4 minutes. Add the spinach, increase the heat to medium and cook, stirring frequently, for 3–4 minutes, or until wilted. Reduce the heat, season to taste with salt and pepper and stir in the flaked almonds.

Beat the eggs with the parsley, water and salt and pepper to taste in a bowl. Pour the mixture into the pan and cook for 5–8 minutes, or until the underside is set. Lift the edge of the tortilla occasionally to allow the uncooked egg to run underneath. Meanwhile, preheat the grill to high.

Sprinkle the grated cheese over the tortilla and cook under the preheated hot grill for 3 minutes, or until the top is set and the cheese has melted. Serve, lukewarm or cold, cut into thin wedges.

aubergine tortilla wedges

SERVES 8–10
as part of a tapas meal

500 g/1 lb 2 oz aubergines
8 tbsp Spanish olive oil
1 onion, chopped
6 eggs
salt and pepper
chopped fresh flat-leaf parsley,
   to garnish (optional)

Cut the aubergines into 5-mm/¹/₄-inch thick slices. Heat 2 tablespoons of the oil in a large frying pan, add the onion and cook over a medium heat, stirring occasionally, for 5 minutes, or until softened but not browned. Add the remaining oil to the frying pan and heat until hot. Add the aubergine slices and cook over a medium heat, turning occasionally, for 15–20 minutes until tender.

Meanwhile, lightly beat the eggs in a large bowl and season generously with salt and pepper. When the aubergines are cooked, drain in a sieve set over a large bowl to catch the oil. When well drained, gently stir into the beaten eggs. Wipe the frying pan clean or wash, if necessary, to prevent the tortilla from sticking. Pour the reserved oil into the frying pan and heat. Add the egg and aubergine mixture and cook gently for 3–4 minutes until the underside is just set and lightly browned. Use a spatula to loosen the tortilla away from the side and base of the pan to allow most of the uncooked egg to run underneath and prevent the tortilla from sticking to the base.

Cover the tortilla with a large, upside-down plate and invert the tortilla onto it. Slide the tortilla back into the frying pan, cooked-side up, and cook for a further 3–4 minutes until the underside is lightly browned.

Slide the tortilla onto a warmed serving dish. Cut the tortilla into wedges and serve warm, sprinkled generously with chopped parsley, if using.

devilled eggs

To cook the eggs, place them in a saucepan, cover with cold water and slowly bring to the boil. Immediately reduce the heat to very low, cover and simmer gently for 10 minutes. As soon as the eggs are cooked, drain and place under cold running water until they are cold. By doing this quickly, it will prevent a black ring from forming around the egg yolk. Gently tap the eggs to crack the eggshells and leave until cold. When cold, crack the shells and remove them.

Using a stainless steel knife, halve the eggs lengthways, then carefully remove the yolks. Place the yolks in a nylon sieve set over a bowl and rub through, then mash them with a wooden spoon or fork. If necessary, rinse the egg whites under cold running water and dry very carefully.

Place the pimientos on kitchen paper to dry well, then chop them finely, reserving a few strips. Finely chop half of the olives. Halve the remaining olives and reserve. If you are going to pipe the filling into the eggs, you need to chop both these ingredients very finely so that they will go through a 1-cm/½-inch nozzle. Add the chopped pimientos and chopped olives to the mashed egg yolks. Add the mayonnaise, mix together well, then add the Tabasco, cayenne and salt and pepper to taste.

For a grand finale, place the egg yolk mixture into a piping bag fitted with a 1-cm/½-inch plain nozzle and pipe the mixture into the hollow egg whites. Alternatively, for a simpler finish, use a teaspoon to spoon the prepared filling into each egg half.

Arrange the eggs on a serving plate. Add 1–2 small strips of the reserved pimientos and an olive half to the top of each stuffed egg. Dust with a little paprika, garnish with lettuce leaves and serve.

SERVES 8
as part of a tapas meal

8 large eggs
2 whole canned or bottled
   pimientos del piquillo
16 stoned green Spanish olives
5 tbsp mayonnaise
8 drops of Tabasco sauce
large pinch of cayenne pepper
salt and pepper
paprika, for dusting
lettuce leaves, to garnish

stuffed eggs with anchovies & cheese

SERVES 8
as part of a tapas meal

8 eggs
50 g/1³/₄ oz canned anchovy
   fillets in olive oil, drained
55 g/2 oz Manchego cheese,
   grated
4 tbsp Spanish extra virgin
   olive oil
1 tbsp freshly squeezed lemon
   juice
1 garlic clove, crushed
salt and pepper
4 stoned green Spanish olives,
   halved
4 stoned black Spanish olives,
   halved
hot or sweet smoked Spanish
   paprika, for dusting

Put the eggs in a saucepan, cover with cold water and slowly bring to the boil. Reduce the heat and simmer gently for 10 minutes. Immediately drain the eggs and rinse under cold running water to cool. Gently tap the eggs to crack the shells and leave until cold.

When the eggs are cold, crack the shells all over and remove them. Using a stainless steel knife, halve the eggs, carefully remove the egg yolks and put in a food processor.

Add the anchovy fillets, Manchego cheese, oil, lemon juice and garlic to the egg yolks and process to a purée. Season to taste with salt and pepper.

Using a teaspoon, spoon the mixture into the egg white halves. Alternatively, using a piping bag fitted with a 1-cm/¹/₂-inch plain nozzle, pipe the mixture into the egg white halves. Arrange the eggs in a serving dish, cover and chill in the refrigerator until ready to serve.

To serve, put an olive half on the top of each stuffed egg and dust with paprika.

eggs & cheese

SERVES 6
as part of a tapas meal

6 hard-boiled eggs, cooled and
  shelled
3 tbsp grated Manchego or
  Cheddar cheese
1–2 tbsp mayonnaise
2 tbsp snipped fresh chives
1 fresh red chilli, deseeded and
  finely chopped
salt and pepper
lettuce leaves, to serve

Cut the eggs in half lengthways and, using a teaspoon, carefully scoop out the yolks into a fine sieve, reserving the egg white halves. Rub the yolks through the sieve into a bowl and add the grated cheese, mayonnaise, chives, chilli and salt and pepper to taste.

Spoon the filling into the egg white halves.

Arrange a bed of lettuce on individual serving plates and top with the eggs. Cover and leave to chill until ready to serve.

asparagus & fried eggs

Trim and discard the coarse, woody ends of the asparagus spears. Make sure all the stems are about the same length, then tie them together loosely with clean kitchen string. If you have an asparagus steamer, you don't need to tie the stems together – just place them in the basket.

Bring a tall saucepan of lightly salted water to the boil. Add the asparagus, making sure that the tips are protruding above the water, reduce the heat and leave to simmer for 10–15 minutes, or until tender. Test by piercing a stem just above the water level with the point of a sharp knife.

Meanwhile, heat a little of the olive oil in a large, heavy-based frying pan. Add 2 eggs, if there is enough room, and fry over a medium-low heat until the whites are just set and the yolks are still runny. Transfer to warmed serving plates and cook the remaining eggs in the same way.

Drain the asparagus and divide the spears among the plates. Serve immediately.

SERVES 6
as part of a tapas meal

500 g/1 lb 2 oz asparagus
   spears
2 tbsp Spanish olive oil
6 eggs

asparagus scrambled eggs

SERVES 6
as part of a tapas meal

450 g/1 lb asparagus, trimmed
   and roughly chopped
2 tbsp Spanish olive oil
1 onion, finely chopped
1 garlic clove, finely chopped
6 eggs
1 tbsp water
salt and pepper
6 small slices country bread

Steam the asparagus pieces for 8 minutes or cook in a large saucepan of boiling salted water for 4 minutes, or until just tender, depending on their thickness. Drain well, if necessary.

Meanwhile, heat the oil in a large frying pan, add the onion and cook over a medium heat, stirring occasionally, for 5 minutes, or until softened but not browned. Add the garlic and cook, stirring, for 30 seconds until softened.

Stir the asparagus into the frying pan and cook, stirring occasionally, for 3–4 minutes. Meanwhile, break the eggs into a bowl, add the water and beat together. Season to taste with salt and pepper.

Preheat the grill to high. Add the beaten eggs to the asparagus mixture and cook, stirring constantly, for 2 minutes, or until the eggs have just set. Remove from the heat.

Toast the bread slices under the grill until golden brown on both sides. Pile the scrambled eggs on top of the toast and serve immediately.

basque scrambled eggs

SERVES 4–6
as part of a tapas meal

2–4 tbsp Spanish olive oil
1 large onion, chopped finely
1 large red pepper, cored,
    deseeded and chopped
1 large green pepper, cored,
    deseeded and chopped
2 large tomatoes, peeled,
    deseeded and chopped
55 g/2 oz chorizo sausage,
    sliced thinly, casings
    removed, if preferred
35 g/1¼ oz butter
10 large eggs, beaten lightly
salt and pepper
4–6 thick slices country-style
    bread, toasted, to serve

Heat 2 tablespoons of the oil in a large, heavy-based frying pan over a medium-high heat. Add the onion and peppers and cook for about 5 minutes, or until the vegetables are soft, but not brown. Add the tomatoes and heat through. Transfer to a plate and keep warm in a preheated low oven.

Add another tablespoon of oil to the frying pan. Add the chorizo and cook for 30 seconds, just to warm through and flavour the oil. Add the sausage to the reserved vegetables.

There should be about 2 tablespoons of oil in the frying pan, so add a little extra, if necessary, to make up the amount. Add the butter and allow to melt. Season the eggs with salt and pepper to taste, then add to the frying pan and scramble until cooked to the desired degree of firmness. Return the vegetables to the frying pan and stir through. Serve at once with hot toast.

flamenco eggs

Preheat the oven to 180°C/350°F/Gas Mark 4. Heat the olive oil in a large, heavy-based frying pan. Add the onion and garlic and cook over a low heat, stirring occasionally, for 5 minutes, or until softened. Add the red peppers and cook, stirring occasionally, for a further 10 minutes. Stir in the tomatoes and parsley, season to taste with salt and cayenne and cook for a further 5 minutes. Stir in the sweetcorn and remove the frying pan from the heat.

Divide the mixture among 4 individual ovenproof dishes. Make a hollow in the surface of each using the back of a spoon. Break an egg into each depression.

Bake in the preheated oven for 15–25 minutes, or until the eggs have set. Serve hot.

SERVES 4
as part of a tapas meal

4 tbsp Spanish olive oil
1 onion, thinly sliced
2 garlic cloves, finely chopped
2 small red peppers, deseeded
  and chopped
4 tomatoes, peeled, deseeded
  and chopped
1 tbsp chopped fresh parsley
salt and cayenne pepper
200 g/7 oz canned sweetcorn
  kernels, drained
4 eggs

baked tomato nests

SERVES 4
as part of a tapas meal

4 large ripe tomatoes
salt and pepper
4 large eggs
4 tbsp double cream
4 tbsp grated aged Mahon,
    Manchego or Parmesan
    cheese

Preheat the oven to 180°C/350°F/Gas Mark 4. Cut a slice off the tops of the tomatoes and, using a teaspoon, carefully scoop out the pulp and seeds without piercing the shells. Turn the tomato shells upside down on kitchen paper and leave to drain for 15 minutes. Season the insides of the shells with salt and pepper.

Place the tomatoes in an ovenproof dish just large enough to hold them in a single layer. Carefully break 1 egg into each tomato shell, then top with 1 tablespoon of cream and 1 tablespoon of grated cheese.

Bake in the preheated oven for 15–20 minutes, or until the eggs are just set. Serve hot.

cheese puffs with fiery tomato salsa

SERVES 8
as part of a tapas meal

70 g/2¹/₂ oz plain flour
50 ml/2 fl oz Spanish olive oil
150 ml/5 fl oz water
2 eggs, beaten
55 g/2 oz Manchego, Parmesan,
  Cheddar, Gouda or Gruyère
  cheese, finely grated
¹/₂ tsp paprika
salt and pepper
sunflower oil, for deep-frying

for the fiery tomato salsa
2 tbsp Spanish olive oil
1 small onion, finely chopped
1 garlic clove, crushed
splash of dry white wine
400 g/14 oz canned chopped
  tomatoes
1 tbsp tomato purée
¹/₄–¹/₂ tsp chilli flakes
dash of Tabasco sauce
pinch of sugar
salt and pepper

To make the salsa, heat the olive oil in a saucepan. Add the onion and fry for 5 minutes, or until softened but not browned. Add the garlic and fry for a further 30 seconds. Add the wine and allow to bubble, then add all the remaining salsa ingredients to the saucepan and simmer, uncovered, for 10–15 minutes, or until a thick sauce has formed. Spoon into a serving bowl and reserve until ready to serve.

Meanwhile, prepare the cheese puffs. Sift the flour on to a plate or sheet of greaseproof paper. Place the olive oil and water in a saucepan and slowly bring to the boil. As soon as the water boils, remove from the heat and quickly add the flour all at once. Using a wooden spoon, beat the mixture until it is smooth and leaves the sides of the saucepan.

Leave the mixture to cool for 1–2 minutes, then gradually add the eggs, beating hard after each addition and keeping the mixture stiff. Add the cheese and paprika, season to taste with salt and pepper and mix well. Store in the refrigerator until you are ready to fry the cheese puffs.

Just before serving the cheese puffs, heat the sunflower oil in a deep-fat fryer to 180–190°C/350–375°F, or until a cube of bread browns in 30 seconds. Drop teaspoonfuls of the prepared mixture, in batches, into the hot oil and deep-fry for 2–3 minutes, turning once, or until golden brown and crispy. They should rise to the surface of the oil and puff up. Drain well on kitchen paper.

Serve the puffs piping hot, accompanied by the fiery salsa for dipping and wooden cocktail sticks to spear the puffs.

fried manchego cheese

Slice the cheese into triangular shapes about 2 cm/³/₄ inch thick or
alternatively into cubes measuring about the same size. Place the flour
in a polythene bag and season to taste with salt and pepper. Break the
egg into a shallow dish and beat together with the water. Spread the
breadcrumbs onto a large plate.

Toss the cheese pieces in the flour so that they are evenly coated,
then dip the cheese in the egg mixture. Finally, dip the cheese in the
breadcrumbs so that the pieces are coated on all sides. Transfer to a
large plate and store in the refrigerator until you are ready to serve
them.

Just before serving, heat about 2.5 cm/1 inch of the sunflower oil in a
large, heavy-based frying pan or deep-fat fryer to 180–190°C/350–375°F,
or until a cube of bread browns in 30 seconds. Add the cheese pieces, in
batches of about 4 or 5 pieces so that the temperature of the oil does
not drop, and deep-fry for 1–2 minutes, turning once, until the cheese is
just beginning to melt and they are golden brown on all sides. Do make
sure that the oil is hot enough, otherwise the coating on the cheese will
take too long to become crisp and the cheese inside may ooze out.

Using a slotted spoon, remove the fried cheese from the frying pan
or deep-fat fryer and drain well on kitchen paper. Serve the fried cheese
pieces hot, accompanied by wooden cocktail sticks on which to spear
them.

SERVES 6–8
as part of a tapas meal

200 g/7 oz Manchego cheese
3 tbsp plain flour
salt and pepper
1 egg
1 tsp water
85 g/3 oz fresh white or brown
  breadcrumbs
sunflower oil, for deep-frying

peppers with fiery cheese

SERVES 6
as part of a tapas meal

1 red pepper, halved and
   deseeded
1 orange pepper, halved and
   deseeded
1 yellow pepper, halved and
   deseeded
115 g/4 oz Afuega'l Pitu cheese
   or other hot spiced cheese,
   diced
1 tbsp clear honey
1 tbsp sherry vinegar
salt and pepper

Preheat the grill to high. Place the peppers, skin-side up, in a single layer on a baking sheet. Cook under the hot grill for 8–10 minutes, or until the skins have blistered and blackened. Using tongs, transfer to a polythene bag, tie the top and leave to cool.

When the peppers are cool enough to handle, peel off the skin with your fingers or a knife and discard it. Place the peppers on a serving plate and sprinkle over the cheese.

Whisk the honey and vinegar together in a bowl and season to taste with salt and pepper. Pour the dressing over the peppers, cover and leave to chill until ready to serve.

empanadillas with cheese & olives

SERVES 6
as part of a tapas meal

85 g/3 oz firm or soft cheese
85 g/3 oz stoned green Spanish
  olives
55 g/2 oz sun-dried tomatoes
  in oil, drained
50 g/1³/₄ oz canned anchovy
  fillets, drained
pepper
55 g/2 oz sun-dried tomato
  paste
500 g/1 lb 2 oz ready-made puff
  pastry, thawed if frozen
plain flour, for dusting
beaten egg, for glazing

Preheat the oven to 200°C/400°F/Gas Mark 6. Cut the cheese into small dice measuring about 5 mm/¹/₄ inch. Chop the olives, sun-dried tomatoes and anchovies into pieces about the same size as the cheese. Place all the chopped ingredients in a bowl, season to taste with pepper and gently mix together. Stir in the sun-dried tomato paste.

Thinly roll out the puff pastry on a lightly floured work surface. Using a plain, round 8-cm/3¹/₄-inch cutter, cut into 16 rounds. Gently pile the trimmings together, roll out again, then cut out a further 8 rounds. Using a teaspoon, place a little of the prepared filling equally in the centre of each of the pastry rounds.

Dampen the edges of the pastry with a little water, then bring up the sides to completely cover the filling and pinch the edges together with your fingers to seal them. With the point of a sharp knife, make a small slit in the top of each pastry. You can store the pastries in the refrigerator at this stage until you are ready to bake them.

Place the pastries onto dampened baking trays and brush each with a little beaten egg to glaze. Bake in the preheated oven for 10–15 minutes, or until golden brown, crisp and well risen. Serve the empanadillas piping hot, warm or cold.

sun-dried tomato
& goat's cheese tarts

Preheat the oven to 220°C/425°F/Gas Mark 7. Dampen a large baking sheet. Finely chop the sun-dried tomatoes and reserve. Heat 1 tablespoon of the reserved oil from the tomatoes in a large frying pan, add the courgette slices and cook over a medium heat, stirring occasionally, for 8–10 minutes until golden brown on both sides. Add the garlic and cook, stirring, for 30 seconds. Remove from the heat and leave to cool while you prepare the pastry bases.

Thinly roll out the pastry on a lightly floured work surface. Using a plain, 9-cm/3¹/₂-inch cutter, cut out 12 rounds, re-rolling the trimmings as necessary. Transfer the rounds to the prepared baking sheet and prick 3–4 times with the tines of a fork. Divide the courgette mixture equally among the pastry rounds, add the tomatoes, leaving a 1-cm/¹/₂-inch border around the edge, and top each tart with a spoonful of goat's cheese. Drizzle over 1 tablespoon of the remaining oil from the tomatoes and season to taste with salt and pepper.

Bake the tarts in the preheated oven for 10–15 minutes until golden brown and well risen. Serve warm.

SERVES 6
as part of a tapas meal

70 g/2¹/₂ oz sun-dried tomatoes
   in oil, drained and 2 tbsp oil
   reserved
1 courgette, thinly sliced
1 garlic clove, crushed
250 g/9 oz puff pastry,
   thawed if frozen
plain flour, for dusting
150 g/5¹/₂ oz soft goat's cheese
salt and pepper

figs with blue cheese

SERVES 6
as part of a tapas meal

for the caramelized almonds
100 g/3¹/₂ oz caster sugar
115 g/4 oz blanched whole
   almonds
butter, for greasing

12 ripe figs
350 g/12 oz Spanish blue
   cheese, such as Picós,
   crumbled
Spanish extra virgin olive oil,
   for drizzling

First make the caramelized almonds. Place the sugar in a saucepan over a medium heat and stir until the sugar melts and turns golden brown and bubbles. Do not stir once the mixture begins to bubble. Remove the saucepan from the heat, add the almonds one at a time and quickly turn with a fork until coated. If the caramel hardens, return the saucepan to the heat. Transfer each almond to a lightly greased baking sheet once it is coated. Leave until cool and firm.

To serve, slice the figs in half and arrange 4 halves on individual serving plates. Roughly chop the almonds by hand. Place a mound of blue cheese on each plate and sprinkle with chopped almonds. Drizzle the figs very lightly with the olive oil.

blue cheese & bean salad

SERVES 4
as part of a tapas meal

150 g/5¹/₂ oz small dried
 haricot beans, soaked for
 4 hours or overnight
1 bay leaf
4 tbsp Spanish olive oil
2 tbsp sherry vinegar
2 tsp clear honey
1 tsp Dijon mustard
salt and pepper
2 tbsp toasted flaked almonds
200 g/7 oz Cabrales or other
 blue cheese, crumbled

Drain the beans and place in a large, heavy-based saucepan. Pour in enough water to cover, add the bay leaf and bring to the boil. Boil for 1–1¹/₂ hours, or until tender, then drain, turn into a bowl and leave to cool slightly. Remove and discard the bay leaf.

Meanwhile, make the dressing. Whisk the olive oil, vinegar, honey and mustard together in a bowl and season to taste with salt and pepper. Pour the dressing over the beans and toss lightly. Add the almonds and toss lightly again. Leave to cool to room temperature.

Spoon the beans into individual serving bowls and scatter over the cheese before serving.

bread

Bread and tapas are a culinary marriage made in heaven. Spaniards don't consider a meal complete without bread, and tapas are no exception. In Barcelona, for example, it's second nature to have a slice of Tomato Bread when stopping at a bar. Visit any tapas bar throughout the country and there will be a selection of salads on bread – creamy mayonnaise-based salads, such as tuna salad, potato salad, Russian salad (a mix of finely diced vegetables) or tender flakes of salt cod. In this chapter you will find plenty of ideas for quick and easy toast toppings as well as a selection of delicious dips and pâtés. There are also recipes for Spanish-style flatbreads and pizzas, not to mention Chorizo Bread Parcels – tiny balls of dough with a meaty filling.

catalan toasts

SERVES 8
as part of a tapas meal

2 garlic cloves
2 large tomatoes
pepper
8 slices day-old French bread
or small rounds country
bread or sourdough bread,
about 2 cm/¾ inch thick
choice of toppings such as
slices of Serrano ham, slices
of Manchego cheese or
pieces of roasted red pepper
(optional)
3 tbsp Spanish extra virgin
olive oil

Preheat the grill to high. Halve the garlic cloves. Coarsely grate the
tomatoes into a bowl, discarding the skins left in your hand, and season
to taste with pepper.

Toast the bread slices under the grill until lightly golden brown on both
sides. While the bread slices are still warm, rub with the cut side of the
garlic halves to flavour, then top with the grated tomatoes. If using, add
a slice of ham or Manchego cheese or a piece of roasted red pepper.
Drizzle each with a little of the oil and serve immediately.

chorizo bread parcels

SERVES 4
as part of a tapas meal

200 g/7 oz strong white flour,
   plus extra for dusting
1¹/₂ tsp easy-blend dried yeast
¹/₂ tsp salt
¹/₄ tsp caster sugar
125 ml/4 fl oz warm water
sunflower oil, for oiling
115 g/4 oz chorizo sausage,
   outer casing removed
aïoli (see page 50), to serve
(optional)

To make the bread dough, put the flour, yeast, salt and sugar in a large bowl and make a well in the centre. Pour the water into the well and gradually mix in the flour from the side. Using your hands, mix together to form a soft dough that leaves the side of the bowl clean.

Turn the dough onto a lightly floured work surface and knead for 10 minutes, or until smooth and elastic and no longer sticky. Shape the dough into a ball and put in a clean bowl. Cover with a clean, damp tea towel and leave in a warm place for 1 hour, or until the dough has risen and doubled in size.

Preheat the oven to 200°C/400°F/Gas Mark 6. Oil a baking sheet. Cut the chorizo sausage into 16 equal-sized chunks. Turn out the risen dough onto a lightly floured work surface and knead lightly for 2–3 minutes to knock out the air.

Divide the dough into 16 equal-sized pieces. Shape each piece into a ball and roll out on a lightly floured work surface to a 12-cm/4¹/₂-inch round. Put a piece of chorizo on each round, gather the dough at the top, enclosing the chorizo, and pinch the edges together well to seal. Put each dough parcel, pinched-side down, on the prepared baking sheet.

Bake in the preheated oven for 20 minutes until pale golden brown. Turn the parcels over so that the pinched ends are facing up and arrange in a serving basket. Serve hot, as soon after baking as possible, as the parcels become dry on standing, accompanied by a bowl of aïoli for dipping, if using.

spicy fried bread
& chorizo

Cut the chorizo into 1-cm/½-inch thick slices and cut the bread, with its crusts still on, into 1-cm/½-inch cubes. Add enough olive oil to a large, heavy-based frying pan to generously cover the base. Heat the oil, add the garlic and fry for 30 seconds–1 minute, or until lightly browned.

Add the bread cubes to the pan and fry, stirring constantly, until golden brown and crisp. Add the chorizo slices and fry for 1–2 minutes, or until hot. Using a slotted spoon, remove the bread cubes and chorizo from the frying pan and drain well on kitchen paper.

Turn the fried bread and chorizo into a warmed serving bowl, add the chopped parsley and toss together. Garnish the dish with a sprinkling of paprika and serve warm. Accompany with wooden cocktail sticks so that a piece of sausage and a cube of bread can be speared together for eating.

SERVES 6–8
as part of a tapas meal

200 g/7 oz chorizo sausage,
  outer casing removed
4 thick slices 2-day-old country
  bread
Spanish olive oil, for pan-frying
3 garlic cloves, finely chopped
2 tbsp chopped fresh flat-leaf
  parsley
paprika, to garnish

chorizo & quail egg toasts

SERVES 6
as part of a tapas meal

12 slices French bread, sliced
    on the diagonal, about
    5 mm/¼ inch thick
about 40 g/1½ oz cured,
    ready-to-eat chorizo, cut into
    thin slices
olive oil
12 quail eggs
mild paprika
salt and pepper

Preheat the grill to high. Arrange the slices of bread on a baking sheet and grill until golden brown on both sides.

Cut or fold the chorizo slices to fit on the toasts; set aside. Heat a thin layer of oil in a large frying pan over a medium heat until a cube of day-old bread sizzles – this takes about 40 seconds. Break the eggs into the frying pan and fry, spooning the fat over the yolks, until the whites are set and the yolks are cooked to your liking.

Remove the fried eggs from the frying pan and drain on kitchen paper. Immediately transfer to the chorizo-topped toasts and dust with paprika. Sprinkle with salt and pepper to taste, and serve at once.

salt cod on garlic toasts

SERVES 6
as part of a tapas meal

200 g/7 oz dried salt cod
5 garlic cloves
225 ml/8 fl oz olive oil
225 ml/8 fl oz double cream
pepper
6 thick slices country bread

Soak the dried salt cod in cold water for 48 hours, changing the water 3 times a day. Drain well, then cut into chunks and place in a large, shallow frying pan. Pour in enough cold water to cover and bring to a simmer. Poach for 8–10 minutes, or until tender. Drain well and leave until cool enough to handle.

Finely chop 4 of the garlic cloves. Halve the remaining clove and reserve until required.

Remove and discard the skin from the fish. Roughly chop the flesh and place in a food processor or blender.

Pour the olive oil into a saucepan and add the chopped garlic. Bring to a simmer over a low heat. Pour the cream into a separate saucepan and bring to simmering point over a low heat. Remove both saucepans from the heat.

Process the fish briefly. With the motor still running, add a little of the garlic oil and process. With the motor still running, add a little cream and process. Continue in this way until all the garlic oil and cream have been incorporated. Scrape the mixture into a serving bowl and season to taste with pepper.

Toast the bread on both sides, then rub each slice with the cut sides of the reserved garlic. Pile the fish mixture onto the toasts and serve.

prawn & haricot toasties

Halve 1 of the garlic cloves and reserve. Finely chop the remaining cloves. Heat 2 tablespoons of the olive oil in a large, heavy-based frying pan. Add the chopped garlic and onion and cook over a low heat, stirring occasionally, for 5 minutes, or until softened.

Stir in the beans and tomatoes and season to taste with salt and pepper. Cook gently for a further 5 minutes.

Meanwhile, toast the bread on both sides, then rub each slice with the cut sides of the reserved garlic and drizzle with the remaining oil.

Stir the prawns into the bean mixture and heat through gently for 2–3 minutes. Pile the bean and prawn mixture onto the toasts and serve immediately, garnished with watercress.

SERVES 4
as part of a tapas meal

3 garlic cloves
4 tbsp Spanish olive oil
1 Spanish onion, halved and
  finely chopped
400 g/14 oz canned haricot
  beans, drained and rinsed
4 tomatoes, diced
salt and pepper
4 thick slices country bread
280 g/10 oz cooked peeled
  prawns
watercress, to garnish

roman dip with anchovy rounds

SERVES 12
as part of a tapas meal

1 egg
150 g/5¹/2 oz stoned black
   Spanish olives
50 g/1³/4 oz canned anchovy
   fillets in olive oil, drained and
   oil reserved
2 garlic cloves, 1 crushed and
   1 peeled but kept whole
1 tbsp capers
¹/2 tsp hot or sweet smoked
   Spanish paprika
1 tbsp Spanish brandy or sherry
4 tbsp Spanish extra virgin
   olive oil
pepper
1 small French bread

Put the egg in a saucepan, cover with cold water and slowly bring to the boil. Reduce the heat and simmer gently for 10 minutes. Immediately drain the egg and rinse under cold running water to cool. Gently tap the egg to crack the shell and leave until cold.

When the egg is cold, crack the shell all over and remove it. Put the egg in a food processor and add the olives, 2 of the anchovy fillets, the crushed garlic, capers, paprika and brandy and process to a rough paste. With the motor running, very slowly add 1 tablespoon of the reserved oil from the anchovies and the extra virgin olive oil in a thin, steady stream. Season the dip to taste with pepper.

Turn the dip into a small serving bowl, cover and chill in the refrigerator until ready to serve. To make the anchovy rounds, put the remaining anchovy fillets, remaining reserved oil from the anchovies and garlic clove in a mortar and, using a pestle, pound together to a paste. Turn the paste into a bowl, cover and chill in the refrigerator until ready to serve.

When ready to serve, preheat the grill to high. Slice the French bread into 2.5-cm/1-inch rounds and toast under the grill until golden brown on both sides. Spread the anchovy paste very thinly on the toasted bread rounds and serve with the dip.

onion & olive rounds

SERVES 4–8
as part of a tapas meal

2 tbsp Spanish olive oil
1 onion, thinly sliced
1 garlic clove, finely chopped
2 tsp chopped fresh thyme
salt and pepper
1 small French bread
1 tbsp tapenade or butter
8 canned anchovy fillets in oil,
  drained
12 green Spanish olives stuffed
  with almonds or onion, halved

Heat the olive oil in a heavy-based frying pan. Add the onion and garlic and cook over a low heat, stirring occasionally, for 15 minutes, or until golden brown and very soft. Stir in the thyme and season to taste with salt and pepper.

Meanwhile, cut off and discard the crusty ends of the bread, then cut the loaf into 8 slices. Toast on both sides, then spread one side with tapenade or butter.

Pile the onion mixture on to the slices of toast and top each slice with an anchovy fillet and the olives. Serve hot.

anchovy rolls

Preheat the oven to 220°C/425°F/Gas Mark 7. Lightly grease a baking sheet. Place the anchovies in a small, shallow dish and pour over the milk. Leave to soak for 10–15 minutes. Drain, discarding the milk, and pat dry with kitchen paper.

Spread each bread slice with butter and then with mustard. Sprinkle with the grated cheese. Divide the anchovies among the bread slices and roll up.

Place on the baking sheet, seam-side down, and bake in the preheated oven for 6–7 minutes. Leave to cool slightly, then serve.

SERVES 4
as part of a tapas meal

butter, for greasing and
   spreading
8 salted anchovies
50 ml/2 fl oz milk
4 slices white bread, crusts
   removed
1 tbsp Dijon mustard
2 tbsp grated Manchego or
   Cheddar cheese

salads on bread

**each salad quantity SERVES 6
as part of a tapas meal**

for the potato salad
200 g/7 oz new potatoes,
    scrubbed and boiled
1/2 tbsp white wine vinegar
salt and pepper
3–4 tbsp mayonnaise
2 hard-boiled eggs, shelled and
    finely chopped
2 spring onions, white and
    green parts finely chopped
1 large French bread

for the tuna salad
200 g/7 oz canned tuna in olive
    oil, drained
4 tbsp mayonnaise
2 hard-boiled eggs, shelled and
    finely chopped
1 tomato, grilled and peeled,
    deseeded and very finely
    chopped
2 tsp grated lemon rind,
    or to taste
cayenne pepper, to taste
salt and pepper
1 large French bread
12 anchovy fillets in oil,
    drained, to garnish

To make the potato salad, peel the potatoes as soon as they are cool
enough to handle, then cut into 5-mm/1/4-inch dice. Toss with the vinegar
and season to taste with salt and pepper. Leave to cool completely. Stir in
the mayonnaise, then fold in the eggs and spring onions. Taste and adjust
the seasoning. Cut the bread on a slight diagonal, 5 mm/1/4 inch thick, into
12 slices. Mound the salad onto the bread.

To make the tuna salad, flake the tuna into a bowl. Stir in the
mayonnaise, then fold in the eggs, tomato, lemon rind and cayenne. Taste
and adjust the seasoning. Cut the bread on a slight diagonal, 5 mm/1/4 inch
thick, into 12 slices. Mound the salad on the bread, then top with
anchovy fillets.

flatbread with vegetables & clams

SERVES 4–6
as part of a tapas meal

2 tbsp Spanish extra virgin
 olive oil
4 large garlic cloves, crushed
2 large onions, thinly sliced
10 pimientos del piquillo,
 drained, patted dry and thinly
 sliced
250 g/9 oz shelled baby clams
 in brine (weight in jar),
 drained and rinsed
salt and pepper

for the dough
400 g/14 oz strong white flour,
 plus extra for dusting
1 sachet easy-blend dried yeast
1 tsp salt
1/2 tsp sugar
1 tbsp Spanish olive oil, plus
 extra for oiling
1 tbsp dry white wine
225 ml/8 fl oz warm water

To make the dough, stir the flour, yeast, salt and sugar together in a bowl, making a well in the centre. Add the olive oil and wine to the water, then pour 175 ml/6 fl oz of the liquid into the well. Gradually mix in the flour from the sides, adding the remaining liquid if necessary, until a soft dough forms.

Turn out the dough onto a lightly floured surface and knead until smooth. Shape the dough into a ball. Wash the bowl and rub the inside with olive oil. Return the dough to the bowl and roll it around so that it is lightly coated in oil. Cover the bowl tightly with clingfilm and leave in a warm place until the dough doubles in size.

Heat the olive oil in a large, heavy-based frying pan over a medium heat. Reduce the heat and add the garlic and onions and fry slowly, stirring frequently, for 25 minutes, or until the onions are golden brown but not burned.

Preheat the oven to 230°C/450°F/Gas Mark 8. Transfer the onions to a bowl and leave to cool. Add the pimiento del piquillo strips and clams to the bowl and stir together. Reserve.

Punch the dough and knead quickly on a lightly floured work surface. Cover it with the upturned bowl and leave for 10 minutes, which will make it easier to roll out.

Heavily flour a 32 × 32-cm/12¾ × 12¾-inch shallow baking tray. Roll out the dough to make a 34-cm/13½-inch square and transfer it to the baking tray, rolling the edges to form a thin rim. Prick the base all over with a fork.

Spread the topping evenly over the dough and season to taste with salt and pepper. Bake in the preheated oven for 25 minutes, or until the rim is golden brown and the onion tips are slightly tinged. Transfer to a wire rack to cool completely. Cut into 12–16 slices.

artichoke & pimiento flatbread

To make the bread dough, put the flour, yeast, salt and sugar in a large bowl and make a well in the centre. Mix the water and oil together in a jug, pour into the well and gradually mix in the flour from the side. Using your hands, mix together to form a soft dough that leaves the side of the bowl clean.

Turn out the dough onto a lightly floured work surface and knead for 10 minutes, or until smooth and elastic and no longer sticky. Shape the dough into a ball and put in a clean bowl. Cover with a clean, damp tea towel and leave in a warm place for 1 hour, or until the dough has risen and doubled in size.

Meanwhile, heat 3 tablespoons of the oil in a large frying pan, add the onions and cook over a medium heat, stirring occasionally, for 10 minutes, or until golden brown. Add the garlic and cook, stirring, for 30 seconds until softened. Leave to cool. When cool, stir in the artichoke hearts and pimientos del piquillo, then season to taste with salt and pepper.

Preheat the oven to 200°C/400°F/Gas Mark 6. Oil a large baking sheet. Turn out the risen dough onto a lightly floured surface and knead lightly for 2–3 minutes to knock out the air. Roll out the dough to a 30-cm/ 12-inch square and transfer to the prepared baking sheet.

Brush the remaining oil over the dough and spread the artichoke and pimiento mixture on top. Sprinkle over the olives, if using. Bake in the preheated oven for 20–25 minutes until golden brown and crisp. Cut into 12 slices and serve hot or warm.

SERVES 4–6
as part of a tapas meal

4 tbsp Spanish olive oil, plus
  extra for oiling
2 large onions, thinly sliced
2 garlic cloves, finely chopped
400 g/14 oz canned artichoke
  hearts, drained and quartered
320 g/11¼ oz bottled or canned
  pimientos del piquillo,
  drained and thinly sliced
salt and pepper
40 g/1½ oz stoned black
  Spanish olives (optional)

for the bread dough
400 g/14 oz strong white flour,
  plus extra for dusting
1½ tsp easy-blend dried yeast
1 tsp salt
½ tsp caster sugar
175 ml/6 fl oz warm water
3 tbsp Spanish olive oil

sun-dried tomato
toasts with goat's cheese

SERVES 6
as part of a tapas meal

2 tbsp Spanish extra virgin olive
  oil, plus extra for oiling
225 g/8 oz soft goat's cheese
2 tsp freshly squeezed lemon
  juice
2 garlic cloves, crushed
1 tsp hot or sweet smoked
  Spanish paprika
25 g/1 oz stoned green Spanish
  olives, finely chopped
1 tbsp chopped fresh flat-leaf
  parsley

for the sun-dried tomato toasts
50 g/1³/₄ oz sun-dried tomatoes
  in oil, drained and 3 tbsp oil
  reserved
1 garlic clove, crushed
1 long French bread

Preheat the oven to 200°C/400°F/Gas Mark 6. Generously oil a baking
sheet. To make the toasts, very finely chop the tomatoes and put in a
bowl. Add the reserved oil from the tomatoes and the garlic and mix
together well.

Slice the bread into 1-cm/¹/₂-inch thick slices and spread with the
tomato mixture. Put on the prepared baking sheet and bake in the
preheated oven for 10 minutes, or until golden brown and crisp. Leave to
cool on a wire rack.

To make the dip, put the goat's cheese in a food processor. With the
motor running, add 1 tablespoon of the oil, drop by drop. Using a spatula,
scrape down the side of the bowl. With the motor running again, very
slowly add the remaining oil and the lemon juice in a thin, steady stream.
Add the garlic and paprika and process until well mixed.

Stir the olives and parsley into the dip. Turn the dip into a small serving
bowl, cover and chill in the refrigerator for at least 1 hour before serving.

Serve the dip accompanied by the toasts.

fresh mint & bean pâté

SERVES 12
as part of a tapas meal

800 g/1 lb 12 oz fresh broad
   beans in their pods, shelled
   to give about 350 g/12 oz
225 g/8 oz soft goat's cheese
1 garlic clove, crushed
2 spring onions, finely chopped
1 tbsp Spanish extra virgin olive
   oil, plus extra to serve
grated rind and 2 tbsp lemon
   juice
about 60 large fresh mint
   leaves, about 15 g/¹/₂ oz
   in total
salt and pepper
12 slices French bread

Cook the broad beans in a saucepan of boiling water for 8–10 minutes until tender. Drain well and leave to cool. When the beans are cool enough to handle, slip off their skins and put the beans in a food processor. This is a laborious task, but worth doing if you have the time. This quantity will take about 15 minutes to skin.

Add the goat's cheese, garlic, spring onions, oil, lemon rind and juice and mint leaves to the broad beans and process until well mixed. Season the pâté to taste with salt and pepper. Turn into a bowl, cover and chill in the refrigerator for at least 1 hour before serving.

To serve, preheat the grill to high. Toast the bread slices under the grill until golden brown on both sides. Drizzle a little oil over the toasted bread slices, spread the pâté on top and serve immediately.

aubergine & pepper dip

Preheat the oven to 190°C/ 375°F/Gas Mark 5. Prick the skins of the aubergines and peppers all over with a fork and brush with 1 tablespoon of the olive oil. Place on a baking tray and bake in the preheated oven for 45 minutes, or until the skins are beginning to turn black, the flesh of the aubergine is very soft and the peppers are deflated.

When the vegetables are cooked, place them in a bowl and cover tightly with a clean, damp tea towel. Alternatively, place the vegetables in a polythene bag and leave for about 15 minutes until cool enough to handle.

When the vegetables have cooled, cut the aubergines in half lengthways, carefully scoop out the flesh and discard the skin. Cut the aubergine flesh into large chunks. Remove and discard the stem, core and seeds from the peppers and cut the flesh into large pieces.

Heat the remaining olive oil in a frying pan. Add the aubergine and pepper and fry for 5 minutes. Add the garlic and fry for 30 seconds.

Turn the contents of the frying pan onto kitchen paper to drain, then transfer to a food processor. Add the lemon rind and juice, the chopped coriander, the paprika, and salt and pepper to taste, then process until a speckled purée is formed.

Transfer the aubergine and pepper dip to a serving bowl. Serve warm, at room temperature, or leave to cool for 30 minutes, then leave to chill in the refrigerator for at least 1 hour and serve cold. Garnish with coriander sprigs and accompany with thick slices of bread or toast for dipping.

SERVES 6–8
as part of a tapas meal

2 large aubergines
2 red peppers
4 tbsp Spanish olive oil
2 garlic cloves, roughly
    chopped
grated rind and juice of
    1/2 lemon
1 tbsp chopped fresh coriander,
    plus extra sprigs to garnish
1/2–1 tsp paprika
salt and pepper
bread or toast, to serve

wild mushroom
& aïoli toasts

SERVES 6
as part of a tapas meal

5 tbsp Spanish olive oil
2 large garlic cloves, finely
  chopped
450 g/1 lb wild, exotic or
  cultivated mushrooms, sliced
2 tbsp dry Spanish sherry
4 tbsp chopped fresh flat-leaf
  parsley
salt and pepper
12 slices long, thick crusty
  bread
8 tbsp aïoli (see page 50)

Heat the oil in a large frying pan, add the garlic and cook over a medium heat, stirring, for 30 seconds until softened. Increase the heat to high, add the mushrooms and cook, stirring constantly, until the mushrooms are coated in the oil and all the oil has been absorbed.

Reduce the heat to low and cook for 2–3 minutes until all the juices have been released from the mushrooms. Add the sherry, increase the heat to high again and cook, stirring frequently, for 3–4 minutes until the liquid has evaporated. Stir in the parsley and season to taste with salt and pepper.

Meanwhile, preheat the grill to high. Toast the bread slices under the grill until lightly golden brown on both sides.

Spread the aïoli on top of each toast and top with the cooked mushrooms. Carefully transfer the toasts to a grill rack and cook under the grill until the aïoli starts to bubble. Serve hot.

roasted red peppers on garlic toasts

SERVES 4
as part of a tapas meal

4 thin slices white country
  bread
5 tbsp Spanish olive oil
2 large garlic cloves, crushed
3 large red peppers
pepper
chopped fresh flat-leaf parsley,
  to garnish

Preheat the oven to 230°C/450°F/Gas Mark 8. To make the garlic toasts, halve each bread slice. Put 3 tablespoons of the oil in a bowl and stir in the garlic. Brush each side of the bread slice halves with the oil mixture and transfer to a baking sheet. Bake in the preheated oven for 10–15 minutes until crisp and golden brown. Leave to cool on kitchen paper.

Reduce the oven temperature to 200°C/400°F/Gas Mark 6. Brush the red peppers with the remaining oil and put in a roasting tin. Roast in the oven for 30 minutes, turn over and roast for a further 10 minutes until the skins have blistered and blackened.

Using a slotted spoon, transfer the roasted peppers to a polythene bag and leave for 15 minutes, or until cool enough to handle.

Using a sharp knife or your fingers, carefully peel away the skin from the peppers. Halve the peppers and remove the stems, cores and seeds, then cut each pepper into neat, thin strips.

To serve, arrange the pepper strips on top of the garlic toasts. Season to taste with pepper and sprinkle with chopped parsley to garnish.

tomato bread

If the bread is soft, toast it under a preheated grill until lightly golden on both sides. Rub each slice of bread with half a fresh juicy tomato. If using, sprinkle over the chopped garlic and drizzle the olive oil over the top.

SERVES 4
as part of a tapas meal

4 slices French bread
2 ripe tomatoes, halved
1 garlic clove, finely chopped
   (optional)
2 tbsp Spanish olive oil
   (optional)

asparagus rolls

SERVES 8
as part of a tapas meal

115 g/4 oz butter, softened,
   plus extra for greasing
8 asparagus spears, trimmed
8 slices white bread, crusts
   removed
1 tbsp chopped fresh parsley
finely grated rind of 1 orange
salt and pepper

Preheat the oven to 190°C/375°F/Gas Mark 5 and lightly grease a baking sheet. If woody, peel the asparagus stems, then tie the spears loosely together with clean kitchen string. Blanch in a tall saucepan of boiling water for 3–5 minutes. Drain and refresh under cold running water. Drain again and pat dry with kitchen paper.

Lightly flatten the slices of bread with a rolling pin. Mix 70 g/2½ oz of the butter, the parsley and orange rind together in a bowl and season to taste with salt and pepper. Spread the flavoured butter over the bread slices.

Place an asparagus spear near one edge of a bread slice and roll up. Repeat with the remaining asparagus spears and bread. Place the asparagus rolls, seam-side down, on the baking sheet.

Melt the remaining butter in a small saucepan, then brush it over the asparagus rolls. Bake in the preheated oven for 15 minutes, or until crisp and golden brown. Leave to cool slightly, then serve warm.

spinach & tomato pizzas

SERVES 16
as part of a tapas meal

2 tbsp Spanish olive oil, plus
    extra for brushing and
    drizzling
1 onion, finely chopped
1 garlic clove, finely chopped
400 g/14 oz canned chopped
    tomatoes
125 g/4½ oz fresh baby spinach
salt and pepper
25 g/1 oz pine kernels

for the bread dough
100 ml/3½ fl oz warm water
½ tsp easy-blend dried yeast
pinch of sugar
200 g/7 oz strong white flour,
    plus extra for dusting
½ tsp salt

To make the bread dough, measure the water into a small bowl, sprinkle in the dried yeast and sugar and leave in a warm place for 10–15 minutes, or until frothy.

Meanwhile, sift the flour and salt into a large bowl. Make a well in the centre and pour in the yeast liquid, then mix together with a spoon. Using your hands, work the mixture until it leaves the sides of the bowl clean.

Turn the dough out onto a lightly floured work surface and knead for 10 minutes, or until smooth and elastic and no longer sticky. Shape into a ball and put it in a clean bowl. Cover with a clean, damp tea towel and leave in a warm place for 1 hour, or until it has risen and doubled in size.

To make the topping, heat the olive oil in a large, heavy-based frying pan. Add the onion and fry for 5 minutes, or until softened but not browned. Add the garlic and fry for a further 30 seconds. Stir in the tomatoes and cook for 5 minutes, letting the mixture bubble and stirring it occasionally, until reduced to a thick mixture. Add the spinach leaves and cook, stirring, until they have wilted slightly. Season to taste with salt and pepper.

While the dough is rising, preheat the oven to 200°C/400°F/Gas Mark 6. Brush several baking sheets with olive oil. Turn the dough out onto a lightly floured work surface and knead well for 2–3 minutes to knock out the air bubbles.

Roll out the dough very, very thinly and, using a 6-cm/2½-inch plain, round cutter, cut out 32 rounds. Place on the prepared baking sheets.

Spread each base with the spinach mixture to cover, then sprinkle the pine kernels over the top. Drizzle a little olive oil over each pizza. Bake in the preheated oven for 10–15 minutes, or until the edges of the dough are golden brown. Serve the spinach and tomato pizzas hot.

INDEX